CLASSIC COOKING OF PUNJAB

Also by Jiggs Kalra :

PRASAD : Cooking with Indian Masters

DAAWAT : An Invitation to Indian Cooking

KAMA BHOG : Foods of Love

Classic Cooking
of Punjab

Jiggs Kalra & Pushpesh Pant

with

Raminder Malhotra

Photographs: Ian Pereira

ALLIED PUBLISHERS PRIVATE LIMITED
NEW DELHI MUMBAI KOLKATA CHENNAI NAGPUR
AHMEDABAD BANGALORE HYDERABAD LUCKNOW

ALLIED PUBLISHERS PRIVATE LIMITED

Regd. Off. : 15 J.N. Heredia Marg, Ballard Estate, Mumbai 400001
Prarthna Flats (2nd Floor), Navrangpura, Ahmedabad 380009
3-2-844/6 & 7 Kachiguda Station Road, Hyderabad 500027
16-A Ashok Marg, Patiala House, Lucknow 226001
5th Main Road, Gandhinagar, Bangalore 560009
1/13-14 Asaf Ali Road, New Delhi 110002
17 Chittaranjan Avenue, Kolkata 700072
81 Hill Road, Ramnagar, Nagpur 440010
751 Anna Salai, Chennai 600002

First Edition, 2004
© Jiggs Kalra
© Photographs : Ian Pereira
ISBN 81-7764-566-8

Published by Sunil Sachdev and printed by Ravi Sachdev at Allied Publishers Private Limited
Printing Division, A-104 Mayapuri, Phase II, New Delhi 110064

This book is for

KHUSHWANT SINGH

my guru
who held my hand
and taught me how to write,
and
who has spent his life
trying to obliterate the line
that divides the two Punjabs

ACKNOWLEDGEMENTS

The writing of this book would not have been possible without Pushpesh Pant, the better half of our writing team since the mid-seventies. Between books, we co-scripted two pioneering telescripts, *Daawat*, now a best-selling book, and the much cloned *Zaike ka Safar*. I would like to imagine that ours is the most enduring writing partnership in the culinary world today.

I welcome back to my team Raminder Malhotra, who used to travel with Pushpesh and me, researching India's foods and recipes.

I would like to thank my Publishers, Sunil and Ravi Sachdev, who have courageously given me a contract for over thirty forthcoming books, unique perhaps in the annals of Indian publishing. I am also grateful to Surojit Banerjee, my editor, who patiently bore with us as we tried to achieve flawless recipes. His contribution is monumental.

I wish to especially thank my guardian angel, Jayshree Kurup, who has been nursing me since I suffered a stroke over three years ago. She has spent hours helping me hunt for pictures for this and other books to follow.

As always, my wife, Lovjeet, and my sons Zorawar and Ajit, are a constant source of encouragement in all my endeavours.

JIGGS KALRA

CONTENTS

PUNJAB'S ROBUST REPAST

JIGGS KALRA & PUSHPESH PANT

Punjab, the Land of the Five Rivers. Perhaps, it would be appropriate to call it the Land of Plenty!! The fertility of its fields and the richness of its dairy have been the envy of the sub-continent.

Some of the most evocative hymns in the *Rig-Veda* pray to the Sun and the Rain Gods to ensure a good crop and healthy milch cattle. A verse in the *Yajur-Veda*, composed around 800 BC, is illustrative of the Punjabi Aryans' preoccupation with food: "May I prosper through the sacrifice and have plenty—milk, ghee, honey—and enjoy food with my kith and kin. May I have freedom from hunger and have my bins full—wheat, lentils and all other grains."

Joie de vivre in Punjab means Good Food, Good F—, and Good Fight. The priority has remained undisturbed for thousands of years. Food reigns supreme. *Ann*, or food grain, declared the Aryans is *Brahm*, the supreme cosmic reality, as it sustains life, nourishes the body and mind and makes all else possible and enjoyable.

No Punjabi has ever treated the 'two square meals' as a daily chore. His ancestors considered eating a sacred ritual. *Yajna*, on the macro level, was the offering of food to the deities through the mediatory fire. To cook and to digest is the same thing-*pachan*. This was the performance of the *yajna* on a micro scale. The digestive fire was offered different foods to transform it into subtler substances that sustained life.

The earliest references to the region's food are found in the Vedas, which document the lives of the Aryans in the Punjab. Amazingly, the elements mentioned over 6,000 years ago are still extant in this cuisine. This includes dairy, *dugdh* (milk), *ghrit* (ghee) and *dadhi* (curd), *shak* (leafy green vegetables) and a variety of grain, *godhum*, related to the Persian *gandhum* (wheat), and the broad-band word *dhanya* (paddy and other grains).

Even today, the staple in the Punjab is grains and vegetables in their basic form. For example, even the most elaborate repast is lovingly referred to as *daal-roti* (lentils and bread). And, it goes without saying, even the most affluent would not miss the ambrosial *sarson da saag te makki di roti* (mustard leaf, in combination with radish leaf, spinach, and *bathua*) cooked in earthenware pots and eaten with maize bread.

Ayurvedic texts refer to *vatika*—a dumpling of sun-dried, spice-specked delicacy made with lentil paste—or what we, today, know as the *vadi*. The art of making *vadi* reached its acme in Amritsar, with the arrival of the merchants of Marwar, who were invited by Ram Das, the fourth Guru of the Sikhs, to streamline the trade in the sacred city. There is also reference to *vataka* or *vada*, made of soaked, coarsely ground and fermented *maash* (husked *urad*) *daal* that was the progenitor of the *dahi vada* on this menu.

The unhusked *maash* is the mother of all lentils. *Rajmah* derives from the word *raj maash*, or the regal *maash*. Other pulses mentioned are *chanak* (*channa daal*), and *alisandaga* (identified as *Kabuli* or large *channa*) that is stated to have reached India with Alexander the Great's troops, who came to India via Afghanistan. Rare is an Indian menu without the *Maah di Daal* and *Pindi Channa*.

The emphasis has traditionally been on robust food, prepared with the simplest of ingredients and the simplest of basic techniques. Just as importantly, the texts make it explicit that there were no inhibitions or taboos with regard to consumption of meats. Game is referred to as *jangaal* and is highly recommended as celebratory and tonic foods. *Beerey da*, a famed barbecue in Amritsar, has kept the glow of those ancient embers alive.

The Aryans were a pastoral people. Even today, the people of the Punjab are a proud agrarian community. Their food continues to be robust and they place a premium on quality and purity. This is what the undivided Punjab took pride in.

Punjab—this side of the border or that—is situated at the crossroads of the Silk Route. This allowed the Punjabis—Sikh, Hindu and Muslim—to imbibe diverse culinary influences. They tasted the best of the rest before anyone else on the sub-continent. The proximity with Persia, Afghanistan and Central Asia gave them a taste for fresh and dried fruits and exotic nuts.

Jinney Lahore nahin wekheya, au janamaya hi nahin. "He who has not seen Lahore has not lived at all." Since the days of Maharaja Ranjit Singh, Lahore has not only been the seat of Imperial Power, but a font of cosmopolitan culture.

Between the two wars, this was the Paris of the East. It drew, like the proverbial magnet, scholars and scientists, poets and painters, musicians and dancers, and, above all else, the greatest chefs from all over. This is where the GOOD LIFE was lived. It was during this era that Punjabi food set the standards.

In our times, post-Partition, most people have forgotten the richness and variety of Punjabi cuisine. The cuisine was never 'monolithic'. Once the largest State in the land, Punjab is subdivided into culinary regions, each with a distinct taste. There is the food of the Pothohar Plateau (Rawalpindi and its environs), Peshawar (so wonderfully influenced by Afghanistan and Uzbekistan), Lahore and Amritsar (the tasty melting pot), and Sargodha (famed for its sweets).

The Partition brought an unprecedented influx of Punjabi refugees—and introduced the rest of the nation to Punjabi food. Not in its pristine form, but in a slightly distorted form. This, of course, was the result of their traumatic dislocation.

As soon as these displaced found their feet, the 'restauratization' of the nation began. They spread all over the country, carrying with them their preferences in food and cooking techniques. A string of *dhaaba* sprang up all over the cities and then proliferated along every single highway. They introduced to the nation the joys of *Tandoori* cuisine and pleasures of eating out. This unique roadside eatery was born to cater to the basic food needs of the uprooted. Many of the better *dhaaba* served fare quite close to home cooking, at affordable prices.

As the *dhaabawallah* made good, they 'up-graded' their cuisine, titillating the palate. The modern Punjabi is an intrepid traveller and an adventurous entrepreneur. In the course of his globetrotting, he has acquired the taste for the exotic. The contemporary Punjabi repast aspires to be subtle and sophisticated.

It would be no exaggeration to say that the most stylish and elegant eateries in the country are Punjabi. With the world shrinking and everyone's appetite for new culinary experiences growing, the Punjabi genius for creative cooking is at the forefront of a grand revival of Indian cuisine.

Let's take a look at some of the sub-regions that have contributed to enriching the cuisine of Punjab.

Peshawar. The most north-western of districts in British India, for centuries, thrived as an entre-pot, famous as a market for turbans, cotton cloth, sandals, copperware, baskets and mats. Shaped like a perfect eclipse, its western border is flanked by the Hindu Kush mountains, impregnable but for the famous Khyber Pass, and bounded in the east by the Indus river, Attock and Hazara.

This is Pathan country and the fare is akin to the food eaten in Afghanistan, albeit with better spicing. The market in Peshawar handled, besides large volumes of cambric, silks and indigo, spices that came from Hyderabad (Deccan), saffron from Kashmir, sugar, salt, tea and asafoetida from Delhi. The exports were raisins and dry fruits.

The fauna is meagre and hawking and snaring have been popular to catch game birds. Fishing is abundant in many streams. Peshawar city is a rich fruit belt, surrounded by lush orchards like

Bhana Mari, Deri Bagbanan, Wazir Bagh and Shahi Bagh, bearing peaches, apricots, plums, pomegranates, limes, apples and quinces.

Rawalpindi. South of Hazara and east of the Jhelum, separated from Kashmir with Attock to its west, the district of Rawalpindi is covered with groves of oak, blue pine, olive and chestnut. The flora and fauna are the same as in the other parts of the lower Himalayas. This area has imbibed culinary influences from Kashmir, the North-West Frontier and the plains irrigated by the Indus. The city, situated at the crossroads, had both commercial and strategic significance. The Pothoharis—the denizens of the plateau—had the good fortune of receiving the best produce from all parts of Punjab, and they devoted their energies to epicureanism.

It is said that in the ancient universities of Nalanda and Taxila, it was the doorman—he acquired vast amounts of knowledge just guarding the portals—who conducted the first interview of a scholar aspiring admission. It seems that every Pindiwallah imbibed sufficient culinary lore and kitchen technique to match the chefs elsewhere. This perhaps is the reason that in post-partition India, the best *dhaaba* were spawned by the refugees from this region. Moti Mahal in Delhi's Daryaganj is, arguably, the first *dhaaba* to acquire the status of a gourmet destination.

Baluchistan. Bounded on the south by the Arabian Sea and extending in the north to Afghanistan and NWFP, Baluchistan touches Persia in the West, and Sind and Punjab in the east. It was one of the largest districts in British India, spread over a vast expanse of over 1,30,000 square miles.

Inhabited by rustic tribes, the food in the region has been basic and robust. A popular dish is *Bilthong*, sun-dried yak meat, *churbi*. Breads are made with wheat or *jowar* (barley). Cheeses of different kinds are an integral part of the diet and among the vegetables, onion, garlic and fresh asafoetida stalks are used. Rice and fish are the staple diet along the coast. Among the game birds, chakor and sand grouse are relished.

Amritsar. Shaped like an oblong between the Ravi and Beas rivers, the district lies northeast of Gurdaspur and south-west of Lahore, occupying an area of 1,600 square miles, including the tract known as Manjha. The forests of *dhaak*, baer, mango and jamun abounded in the district until recent urbanisation decimated most of them. The chief crops are wheat, gram, barley, maize, rice, cotton, pulses and sugarcane. The region is famous for its buffaloes and its milk products. And, all these have created a bazaar cuisine so wonderful that fully 50% of its people, it is claimed, dine out every day. The rest 'take-away' and consume it at home!

Famed for the shrine, the Golden Temple, Amritsar is equally renowned as a commercial centre. Caravans from Bukhara, Kabul and Kashmir came here and this was an important outlet to Peshawar and beyond. In the mid-19th Century, there was an exodus of Kashmiri weavers from the Vale after a famine and they settled down in Amritsar. The city soon became famous for its shawls and carpets.

After Partition, the state of Pakistan has been dominated by the West Punjabis, who looked down on tribal minorities and smaller ethnic groups included in the nation. Their food has been denigrated and the *nouveau riche* and the elite have adopted the *haute cuisine* brought by the Mohajir from UP as their own.

The wonderful diversity of the Frontier foods and the rich streams of Hindu/Sikh/Pathan Punjabi cuisine have flown downstream with the exodus of the refugees, who have lovingly cherished and preserved this tradition.

WEIGHTS & MEASURES

The recipes in this book were perfected in the metric measures. The quantities, however, are given in both metric and American measures. As it is difficult to exactly convert from one to the other, adjustments have been made ensuring that the taste would not vary in the slightest.

Fortunately, in Indian cooking a few extra grams of onions or ginger or tomatoes will not make much of a difference. Nor would a few extra millilitres of water. Nevertheless, whenever the recipe has demanded exactness, it has been provided. For example, the reader will occasionally come across something like 3 cups + 4 tsp.

The following chart should help with the conversions :

1 Gram	=	0.035 ounces
10 Grams	=	0.35 ounces
100 Grams	=	3.5 ounces
200 Grams	=	7.0 ounces

To convert grams into ounces, multiply the grams by 0.035.

To give convenient working equivalents, the metric measures have been rounded off into units of 5 or 25 (*see the following chart*).

Ounces	Grams	Nearest Equivalent	Conversion
1	28.35	28	20/30
2	56.70	57	50/60
3	85.05	85	75/90
4	113.40	113	100/120
5	141.75	142	150
6	170.10	170	175
7	198.45	198	200

8	226.80	227	225
9	255.15	255	250
10	283.50	284	275/290
11	311.85	312	300/325
12	340.20	340	350
13	368.55	369	375
14	396.90	397	400
15	425.25	425	425
16 or 1 1b	453.60	454	450

For more convenient conversions, the following chart will be useful :

1 tsp (teaspoon)	=	5g
2 tsp	=	10g
3 tsp	=	15g
1 Tbs (tablespoon)	=	15g
1 Tbs	=	3 tsp or ½ oz
¼ cup	=	4 Tbs or 2 oz
cup	=	5 Tbs + 1 tsp
½ cup	=	8 Tbs or 4 oz
cup	=	10 Tbs + 2 tsp
¾ cup	=	12 Tbs or 6 oz
1 cup	=	16 Tbs or 8 oz
1 cup (liquid measure)	=	237 ml
1 oz (dry measure)	=	28.35g
16 oz (liquid measure)	=	2 cups or 1 pint
2 pints (liquid measure)	=	4 cups or 1 quart

To convert the commonly used ingredients in this book, the following chart will be a convenient guide :

VEGETABLES

Coriander (chopped)	1 cup	60g
	1 Tbs	4g
Green Peas (shelled)	1 cup	160g
Mint (chopped)	1 cup	60g
	1 Tbs	4g

Mushrooms	1 cup	70g
Onions (chopped, diced)	1 cup	170g
Potatoes (diced, cubes)	1 cup	150g
Tomatoes (chopped)	1 cup	225g

LENTILS

All *dals*	1 cup	200g
All dry beans	1 cup	200g
All gram (White, Bengal, etc.)	1 cup	200g

CEREALS

Rice	1 cup	200g
Semolina	1 cup	200g

FLOUR

Atta (whole-wheat flour)	1 cup	120g
Cornflour	1 cup	80g
Gramflour	1 cup	150g
Flour or roasted *channa dal*	1 cup	150g
Flour (all purpose)	1 cup	125g
Breadcrumbs	1 cup	100g

DAIRY

Cheddar Cheese (grated)	1 cup	110g
Cream	1 cup	240ml
Milk	1 cup	240ml
Yoghurt	1 cup	225g
Hung Yoghurt	1 cup	260g

FATS & OILS

Desi Ghee or Clarified Butter	1 cup	225g
	1 Tbs	15g
Ghee or Vegetable Fat	1 cup	200g
	1 Tbs	12½g

White Butter	1 cup	225g
	1 Tbs	15g
Groundnut Oil	1 cup	220ml
	1 Tbs	15ml
Mustard Oil	1 cup	220ml
	1 Tbs	15ml

SUGAR & SPICE

Castor (confectioner's) Sugar	1 cup	120g
	1 Tbs	8g
Granulated Sugar	1 cup	200g
	1 Tbs	12g
Ajwain	1 tsp	2.5g
	1 Tbs	7.5g
Black Onion seeds (*Kalonji*)	1 tsp	3.3g
	1 Tbs	10.0g
Black Peppercorns	1 tsp	3.3g
	1 Tbs	10.0g
Coriander seeds	1 tsp	2.0g
	1 Tbs	6.0g
Cumin seeds	1 tsp	3.0g
	1 Tbs	9.0g
Fennel seeds	1 tsp	2.5g
	1 Tbs	7.5g
Fenugreek seeds	1 tsp	4.5g
	1 Tbs	13.5g
Kasoori Methi (Dry Fenugreek Leaves, broiled and powdered)	1 Tbs	12g
Melon seeds	1 tsp	3.3g
	1 Tbs	10.0g
Pomegranate seeds	1 tsp	3.3g
	1 Tbs	10.0g
Poppy seeds	1 tsp	3.0g
	1 Tbs	9.0g
Sesame seeds	1 tsp	3.5g

	1 Tbs	10.5g
Sunflower seeds	1 tsp	3.3g
	1 Tbs	10.0g
All powdered spices	1 tsp	5g

DRY FRUITS & NUTS

Almonds (blanched, peeled)	1 cup	140g
Cashewnuts (peeled)	1 cup	140g
Coconut (grated)	1 cup	80g
Coconut (dessicated)	1 cup	60g
Peanuts (shelled, peeled)	1 cup	140g
Pistachio (blanched, peeled)	1 cup	140g
Raisins	1 cup	145g
Walnuts (chopped)	1 cup	120g

PASTES

Boiled Onion paste	1 cup	240g
Cashewnut paste	1 cup	250g
Coconut paste	1 cup	260g
Fried Onion paste	1 cup	265g
Garlic paste/Ginger paste	1¾ tsp	10g
	2½ tsp	15g
	4 tsp	25g
	5 tsp	30g
	3 tsp	50g

LIQUIDS

Lemon juice	1 cup	240 ml
Water	1 cup	240 ml

KANJEE

INGREDIENTS

1Kg/2¼ lb Black Carrots
100g/1 cup Mustard Seeds
3g/1tsp Red Chilli Powder
5g/1 tsp Black Pepper
   (freshly broiled and crushed)

3g/1tsp Black Salt Powder
Salt
Earthenware Vessel (*Matka*)
   with lid, 5ltr volume

Serves: 4
Preparation time: 3 days

PREPARATION

The Carrots: Peel, wash and cut into dices.

The Mustard: Soak and make a thick paste.

The Matka: Clean, soak in water, wash and keep aside.

Mix all the ingredients in the matka and leave aside for half an hour. Top the matka with drinking water and cover the mouth with muslin cloth. Keep the earthenware vessel near a warm place for three days.

After three days when the contents of the matka have fermented, strain and refrigerate.

TO SERVE

Garnish with a sprig of mint and serve cold in a Tom Collins.

---•---

SHIKANJVI

INGREDIENTS

1200ml/5cups Chilled Potable Water
120ml/½ cup Lemon Juice
Salt

Sugar
3g/1tsp Black Salt Powder
3g/1tsp Black Pepper Powder

Serves: 4
Preparation Time: 5 minutes

PREPARATION

Add sugar, salt, lemon juice and stir it in. Sprinkle black salt powder and black pepper powder and serve.

———————————————— • ————————————————

LUSSEE

INGREDIENTS

325ml/1¼ cup *Dahi*/Natural Yoghurt
800ml/3½ cup Chilled Water
105g/7Tbsp Granulated Sugar

Crushed Ice
15ml/1Tbsp Rose Syrup

Serves: 4
Preparation Time: 5 minutes

PREPARATION

Put all the ingredients except the ice and rose syrup in a blender and whip at high speed for 2-3 minutes.

TO SERVE

Place some crushed ice into every Tom Collins and pour the whipped up frothy lussee, garnish with a swirl of rose syrup. Serve immediately.

———————————————— • ————————————————

MATTHA/BUTTER MILK

INGREDIENTS

250g/1 cup *Dahi*/Natural Yoghurt
1lt/4¼ cup Chilled Water
3g/1tsp Cumin Seeds (freshly broiled and roasted)
1" Ginger (peeled and chopped fine)
1 Green Chilli (seeded and chopped)

1.5g/½ tsp Red Chilli Powder
4g/2Tbsp Fresh Coriander
   (Cleaned and chopped)
Crushed Ice
Salt

Serves: 4
Preparation Time: 15 minutes

PREPARATION

Put the yoghurt in a food processor. Add the ginger, salt, green chillies, chilled water and mix at high speed for 2 minutes.

TO SERVE

Pour into individual glasses along with crushed ice. Serve garnished with chopped coriander, red chilli powder and freshly broiled cumin powder.

TEH te TEH KEBAB

INGREDIENTS

12 roundels Paneer (3" diameter; ¾" thick)   Salt
3g/1tsp Red Chilli Powder

The Batter

130g/½ cup *Chakka Dahi*/Yoghurt   0.375g/⅛ tsp *Gulaabpankhrhi*/
    Cheese/Hung Yoghurt (whisk)   Rose Petal Powder
Salt   30ml/2 Tbs Cream
3g/1tsp White Pepper Powder

The 1st Filling

15g/5tsp Mustard Seeds   Salt
4 Green Chillies   15ml/1Tbs Cream
5g Ginger (finely chopped)
6.5g/2Tbs *Taaza Dhania*/Coriander
    (finely chop)

The 2nd Filling

16 Walnuts (finely chopped)   1.5g/½ tsp *Chotti Elaichi*/
20g/1½ Tbs Cashew nut (finely chopped)   Green Cardamom Powder
10 Pistachio (finely chopped)   0.75g/¼ tsp *Lavang*/Clove Powder
60g/2oz Grated *Khoya*   30ml/2 Tbsp Cream
45g/1½ oz Cheese   Salt
    (Cheddar/Processed; grated)
3g/1 tsp *Saunf*/Fennel Powder

Serves : 4
Preparation Time : 2 hours
Cooking Time : 4-5 minutes

PREPARATION

THE PANEER: Arrange the roundels on a tray in a single layer, sprinkle salt and red chilli powder. Leave the tray on a table with one side propped up slightly to help drain the residual moisture.

Shikanjvi & Kanjee (*Thirst Quenchers*)

Teh te Teh Kebab (*Kebab*)

Harre Chholia te Khumbwali Seekh (*Kebab*)

Jhangi Champaan (*Stir-fry*)

Lawrence Road Wale Tikkey (*Stir-fry*)

Amritsari Machchi (*Kebab*)

Bhatti da Murg (*Kebab*)

THE 1st FILLING: Soak the mustard seeds in just enough water to cover for 15 minutes. In a food processor add all the ingredients and purée into a smooth paste.

THE 2nd FILLING: Cream the khoya and cheese in a mixing bowl using the palm of your hand adding little cream at a time. Mix in the remaining ingredients to a coarse paste.

THE BATTER: Mix the dried rose petal powder with cream and slowly whisk in with the yoghurt.

THE ASSEMBLING

Spoon dollops of the mustard filling on a roundel of paneer spread evenly and cover with another roundel. Spread a spoonful of the nut paste over the second roundel and place a third roundel on top. Hold these three slices of paneer firmly and dip in the batter. Repeat the procedure with the other slices and arrange on a tray and refrigerate for 10 minutes.

THE SKEWERING: Pierce 2 paneer roundels and small potatoes (to prevent paneer from touching or sliding down), alternately, in a skewer and keep a tray underneath to collect drippings.

COOKING

Roast in moderately hot tandoor for 3-4 minutes, on charcoal grill for 3-4 minutes, in pre-heated oven (275°F) for 7-8 minutes.

TO SERVE

Unskewer paneer and potatoes (discard), arrange paneer on platter and serve hot with Mint Chutney.

———————— • ————————

BHATTI da PANEER

INGREDIENTS

800g/1¾ lb *Paneer* (2" x 2" x 1" Cubes)	3g/1tsp Red Chilli Powder
Desi Ghee/Clarified Butter for basting	Salt

The Marination

45ml/3 Tbs Cooking Oil	1.5g/½ tsp *Chotti Elaichi*/
30g/5¼ tsp Garlic Paste (strain	Green Cardamom Powder
20g/3½ tsp Ginger Paste (strain)	1.5g/½ tsp *Lavang*/Clove Powder

45ml/3 Tbs Yoghurt (whisk)
60ml/¼ cup Malt Vinegar
3g/1 tsp *Jeera*/Cumin Powder
3g/1 tsp *Dhania*/Coriander Powder
3g/1 tsp Black Pepper
 (freshly roasted & coarsely ground)
3g/1 tsp *Kashmiri Deghi Mirch* Powder
1.5g/½ tsp *Daalcheeni*/Cinnamon Powder

0.75g/¼ tsp *Javitri*/Mace Powder
0.375g/⅛ tsp *Jaiphal*/Nutmeg Powder
0.375g/⅛ tsp *Maghay* Powder
A generous pinch of *Kasoori Methi*/
 Dried Fenugreek Leaf Powder
Salt

Serves: 4
Preparation Time: 30 minutes (plus 1 hour marination time)
Cooking Time: 8-10 minutes

PREPARATION

THE PANEER: Arrange the paneer on a tray in a single layer, sprinkle salt and red chilli powder. Leave the tray on a table with one side propped up slightly to help drain the water.

THE MARINATION: Heat oil in a *kadhai*/wok, add garlic and ginger, *bhunno*/stir-fry over medium heat until the moisture evaporates. Remove *kadhai*/wok from heat, stir-in yoghurt, mix well, transfer to a large bowl and cool. When cool, mix the remaining ingredients, smear the paneer with this marinade and reserve in the bowl for an hour.

COOKING

Place the marinated paneer in convenient batches on a charcoal grill and roast over medium heat for 2-3 minutes, turning once, and basting with ghee at regular intervals.

TO SERVE

Unskewer paneer and arrange on platter, serve hot with Mint Chutney.

MULTANI TIKKA

INGREDIENTS

800g/1¾lb Paneer (2" x 2" x 1" Cubes)
The Batter

260g/1 cup *Chakka Dahi*/Yoghurt Cheese/
  Hung Yoghurt
30g/1 oz Green Peppercorns
7g/1 Tbs Rice Flour
3g/1 tsp Red Chilli Powder
2.5g/1 tsp *Ajwain*/Carom Seeds
0.375g/⅛ tsp *Jaiphal*/Nutmeg Powder

0.375g/⅛ tsp *Chotti Elaichi*/
  Green Cardamom Powder
0.375g/⅛ tsp *Gulaabpankhrhi*/
  Rose Petal Powder
Salt
90ml/6 Tbs Single Cream
Generous pinch of *Tandoori Kebab Masala*

PREPARATION

THE BATTER: Whisk yoghurt cheese. Drain green peppercorns, pat dry and finely chop. Sift rice flour, add to yoghurt cheese and whisk to remove lumps. Add remaining ingredients, except cream and kebab masala and whisk again. Fold in cream, dip chunks in this batter, arrange in tray, pour the remaining batter on top of the chunks and reserve in refrigerator for 30 minutes.

THE SKEWERING: Skewer paneer (cottage cheese) chunks in convenient batches and then skewer a raw onion (to prevent paneer from sliding down). Keep a tray underneath to collect drippings.

COOKING

Roast in moderately hot tandoor for 5-6 minutes, on charcoal grill for 6-7 minutes, in pre-heated oven (275°F) for 10-12 minutes.

TO SERVE

Unskewer onions and paneer (cottage cheese), arrange chunks on platter, sprinkle a generous pinch or two of the Tandoori Kebab Masala and serve hot.

BHUTTEYAN da KEBAB

INGREDIENTS

4 *Bhuttey*/Corn Cobs (9"; remove
  kernels, reserve cobs)
4 *Bhuttey*/Sweet Corn Cobs
  (9"; same as above)
720ml/3 cups Milk
Cooking Oil to deep fry *Bhuttey*
100g/3 oz *Besan*/Gramflour
5 Brittania Cheese Slices (mash)
2 Eggs (beat)
60g/2 oz Onions (chop)
10g/1" piece Ginger (finely chop)

8 Green Chillies (seed & chop)
1.5g/½ tsp Black Pepper
  (freshly roasted & coarsely ground)
2g/1 tsp *Jeera*/Cumin Seeds
1.5g/½ tsp *Motti Elaichi*/
  Black Cardamom Powder
0.75g/¼ tsp *Lavang*/Clove Powder
0.75g/¼ tsp *Daalcheeni*/
  Cinnamon Powder
0.375g/⅛ tsp *Jaiphal*/Nutmeg Powder
Salt

Serves: 4
Preparation Time: 1:30 hours
Cooking Time: 4-5 minutes per set

PREPARATION

THE CORN: Put milk in a *handi*/pan, add salt, bring to a boil, add the corn kernels, cook until soft, drain, squeeze dry in a muslin cloth and transfer to a bowl. Add the remaining ingredients to the corn, mix well and divide into 16 equal portions. (The cooking time depends on the age of the corn. Don't be alarmed if the milk and water are completely absorbed. If the corn is soft and milky, you may need lesser quantities of milk and water.)

THE COBS: Remove the stems and the tips and halve. Using a moist hand spread a portion of the corn mixture evenly onto the cob.

COOKING

Heat oil in a *kadhai*/wok and deep fry cobs over medium heat until crisp and golden. Remove to absorbent paper to drain the excess fat.

TO SERVE

Arrange doily paper on a service platter, place the bhuttey on top and serve with Mint Chutney.

HARRE CHHOLIA te KHUMBWALI SEEKH

INGREDIENTS

360g/2¼ cups *Harre Chholia*/
  Fresh Bengal Gram
200g/2 cups Mushrooms (chop)
220g/2 cups *Paneer* (grate)
37.5g/3 Tbs *Desi Ghee*/Clarified Butter
1g/½ tsp *Jeera*/Cumin Seeds
10g/1" piece Ginger (finely chop)

110g/1 cup Processed Cheese (grate)
32 Almonds (blanch, cool, peel &
  cut into slivers)
6.5g/2 Tbs *Taaza Dhania*/Coriander (chop)
6 Green Chillies (seed & finely chop)
Salt

The Masala

3g/1 tsp *Amchoor*/Mango Powder
1.5g/½ tsp Black Pepper (freshly roasted &
  coarsely ground)
0.75g/¼ tsp *Chotti Elaichi*/Green
  Cardamom Powder

0.75g/¼ tsp *Motti Elaichi*/Black
  Cardamom Powder
0.75g/¼ tsp *Javitri*/Mace Powder
A generous pinch of *Kaala Namak*/
  Black Rock Salt Powder

Serves: 4
Preparation Time: 1: 10 hours
Cooking Time: 7-8 minutes

PREPARATION

THE SEEKH MIXTURE: Boil chholia until al dente, drain, cool, transfer to a blender and pulse to obtain a coarse paste. Heat ghee in a *kadhai*/wok, add cumin, stir over medium heat until it begins to pop, add ginger and sauté for a few seconds. Then add mushrooms, *bhunno*/stir-fry until the moisture evaporates, add chholia and *bhunno*/stir fry until the mixture is devoid of moisture and the paste becomes akin to a *khoya* ball. Remove, cool, add the remaining ingredients and divide into 16 equal portions.

THE MASALA: Mix all the spices and keep aside.

THE SKEWERING: Using a moist hand, spread the balls by pressing each along the length of the skewers, two inches apart and making each kebab 6" long.

COOKING

Roast in a moderately hot tandoor for 3-4 minutes or until light brown crust forms on the surface. Or cook on a charcoal grill, for about the same time. The kebab can also be deep-fried in a *kadhai*/wok, in which case you make croquets and don't skewer the mixture. Sprinkle the masala.

———————— • ————————

BHUNEE CHAAT

INGREDIENTS

The Paneer

200g/7 oz *Paneer*/Cottage Cheese (1" cubes)
260g/1 cup *Chakka Dahi*/Yoghurt
   Cheese/Hung Yoghurt
30g/1 oz Green Peppercorns
7g/1 Tbs Rice Flour
3g/1 tsp Yellow Chilli Powder
Salt

2.5g/1 tsp *Ajwain*/Carom Seeds
0.375g/⅛ tsp *Chotti Elaichi*/
   Green Cardamom Powder
0.375g/⅛ tsp *Jaiphal*/Nutmeg Powder
0.375g/⅛ tsp *Gulaabpankhrhi*/
   Rose Petal Powder
90ml/6 Tbs Single Cream

The Fruits & Vegetables

2 Avocado (large; 1" cubes)
1 Lemon (halve)
2 Sweet Potatoes (large; 1" cubes)
1 *Laal Shimla Mirch*/Red Bell
   Pepper (large)
1 *Peeli Shimla Mirch*/Yellow Bell
   Pepper (large)

1 *Harri Shimla Mirch*/Green Bell
   Pepper (large)
4 slices Pineapple (canned; 1" pieces)
Cooking Oil to grease baking tray

The Dressing

45ml/3 Tbs Balsamic Vinegar
60ml/¼ cup Olive/Salad Oil
3g/1 tsp *Kaala Namak*/Black
   Rock Salt Powder
6g/2 tsp *Anaardaana*/Pomegranate Powder

6g/2 tsp *Amchoor*/Mango Powder
2.25g/¾ tsp *Jeera*/Cumin Powder
1.25g/½ tsp *Shahi Jeera*/
   Black Cumin Seeds
Salt

6g/2 tsp Black Pepper Powder
  (coarsely ground)

Serves: 4
Preparation: 1 hour
Cooking Time: 3 minutes

PREPARATION

THE PANEER: Whisk yoghurt cheese in a bowl, add the remaining ingredients, mix well, evenly coat the paneer with this marinade and reserve for 15 minutes.

THE AVOCADO: Boil enough water in a *handi*/pan, add lemon halves and avocado, blanch for 2-3 minutes, drain and refresh in iced water.

THE SWEET POTATO: Boil in salted water until al dente (cooked, but firm and not squishy), drain and cool.

THE BELL PEPPERS: Remove stems, halve, seed and cut into 1" square pieces.

THE DRESSING: Put all the ingredients, except oil, in a bowl, mix well. Then add oil in a steady stream, whisking constantly, until emulsified.

THE MARINATION: Reserve the avocado, sweet potatoes and the remaining fruits and vegetables in the dressing for 15 minutes.

THE SKEWERING: Skewer the ingredients as follows: pineapple, green pepper, paneer, red pepper, avocado, yellow pepper and sweet potato and repeat the sequence in convenient batches. Reserve the dressing.

COOKING

Roast in a moderately hot tandoor, on a charcoal grill, or in the pre-heated oven, for 3 minutes. Remove and keep aside.

TO SERVE

Put equal quantities of paneer, fruits and vegetables in each of 4 individual plates, pour on the reserved dressing and serve as an appetiser.

BHISAN de KEBAB

INGREDIENTS

600g/1 lb 5 oz *Kamal Kakari*/Lotus Root
150g/5 oz Potatoes (boil & grate)
60g/2 oz Cheese (Cheddar/Processed; grate)
4 Green Chillies (seed & finely chop)
6g/2 tsp *Anaardaana*/Pomegranate Powder
3g/1 tsp *Saunf*/Fennel Powder

1.5g/½ tsp *Chotti Elaichi*/
   Green Cardamom Powder
0.75/¼ tsp *Lavang*/Clove Powder
3.25g/1 Tbs *Tulsi*/Basil (fresh; chop)
Salt
Desi Ghee to deep fry kofta

The Filling

100g/3 oz *Paneer* (grate)
12 *Chchuhaara*/Dried Dates
   (remove pits and chop)
8 *Aloobukhara*/Dried Plums
   (remove pits and chop)

32 *Chilgozey*/Pine Nuts
10g/1" piece Ginger
4.5g/1½ tsp Black Pepper
   (freshly roasted & coarsely ground)
Salt

Serves: 4
Preparation Time: 2 hours
Cooking Time: 2-3 minutes

PREPARATION

THE LOTUS ROOT MIXTURE: Wash lotus root in running water to remove grit, peel, grate, boil, drain and squeeze in a cloth napkin to remove the excess moisture. Add the remaining ingredients, mix well, divide into 16 equal portions and make balls.

THE FILLING: Mix all the ingredients and divide into 16 equal portions.

THE STUFFING: Flatten each ball between the palms, place a portion of the filling in the middle, and make balls again and make egg-shapes.

THE FRYING: Heat ghee in a *kadhai*/wok and deep fry egg-shaped kebab over medium heat until light golden. Remove to absorbent paper to drain excess fat.

THE SKEWERING: Skewer the kebab in batches of four and keep aside.

COOKING

Roast in a moderately hot tandoor for approximately 2-3 minutes.

BHARWAAN SHIMLA MIRCH

INGREDIENTS

2 *Laal Shimla Mirch*/ Red Bell Pepper

2 *Harra Shimla Mirch*/ Green Bell Pepper

2 *Peeli Shimla Mirch*/ Yellow Bell Pepper

The Marinade

30ml/2Tbsp Lemon Juice

30ml/2 Tbsp Refined Oil

10g/1¾ tsp Ginger Paste

Salt

15g/2½ tsp Garlic Paste

The Stuffing

5 Medium sized Potatoes

10g/2 tsp Ginger (chopped fine)

10g/5Tbsp Fresh Coriander (chopped fine)

3g/1 tsp *Jeera*/Cumin Seeds

1.5g/½ tsp *Haldee*/Turmeric Powder

4g/1 tsp Black Pepper Powder

3g/ 1 tsp Red Chilli Powder

60ml/4Tbsp Refined oil

100g/4oz *Paneer*/ Cottage cheese (grated)

1g/½ tsp *Rai*/ Black Mustard Seeds

100g/4oz Cheddar (grated)

5ml/1 tsp Lemon Juice

4 Green Chilli (chopped fine)

Serves: 4

Preparation Time: 50 minutes

Cooking Time: 2-3 minutes in a moderately hot tandoor

6-7 minutes in an oven

PREPARATION

The Bell Peppers: Cut the caps, deseed and clean. Mix the marinade and rub the insides of the peppers.

The Potatoes: Peel, wash, cut into ¼ inch dices, wash, and reserve in water.

THE STUFFING

Heat oil, add rai and jeera and sauté till it crackles. Add the potatoes, turmeric powder, red chilli powder and *bhunno*/stir-fry in medium heat till light golden in colour. Add the ginger, green chillies, paneer, coriander and stir for couple of minutes. Sprinkle black pepper powder and lemon juice. Add the cheese, adjust the seasoning and remove.

THE ASSEMBLY

Allow the stuffing to cool and divide into 8 equal portions. Stuff each bell pepper with this stuffing and pack neatly.

THE SKEWERING

Skewer the peppers an inch apart, and then skewer a raw onion to prevent the peppers from sliding down.

COOKING

Roast in a moderately hot tandoor for 5-6 minutes. In a preheated oven for 8-9 minutes.

TO SERVE

Cut into half and serve hot with mint chutney.

BHARWAAN TANDOORI ALOO

INGREDIENTS

12 Potatoes (medium; oblong)

The Filling

2 Potatoes (large; tiny dices)
Cooking Oil to deep fry potatoes
250g/9 oz *Paneer* (grate)
150g/5 oz Cheddar Cheese (grate)
10g/1" piece Ginger (finely chop)
4 Green Chillies (seed & finely chop)
6.5g/2 Tbs *Taaza Dhania*/Coriander (finely chop)
2.25g/¾ tsp Black Pepper (freshly roasted & coarsely ground)

1.5g/½ tsp *Jeera*/Cumin Powder
1.5g/½ tsp *Chotti Elaichi*/Green Cardamom Powder
0.75g/¼ tsp *Lavang*/Clove Powder
0.75g/¼ tsp *Javitri*/Mace Powder
A generous pinch of *Kaala Namak*/Black Rock Salt Powder
Salt
36 Cashewnut Quarters
12 Black Raisins (halve)

Serves: 4
Preparation Time: 1:30 hour
Cooking Time: 4-5 minutes

PREPARATION

THE POTATOES: Scrub or peel (we prefer to keep the skin on). Slice a small piece lengthways (horizontally) and scoop out the centre, leaving ¼" walls on the sides and the base intact. Put the scooped potatoes in a steamer/iddli maker and steam for 15-20 minutes or until al dente (cooked, but firm), remove and cool. (Reserve the scooped potatoes for some other dish.)

THE FILLING: Heat oil in a *kadhai*/wok, add potato dices and deep fry over medium heat until golden. Remove to absorbent paper to drain the excess fat. Once cool, add the remaining ingredients, mix well, but with a soft hand (the mixture should not get mashed) and divide into 12 equal portions.

THE STUFFING: Pack a portion of the filling in each of the potatoes.

THE OVEN: Pre-heat to 350°F.

THE SKEWERING: Skewer potatoes vertically in convenient batches, with a little gap between each.

COOKING

Roast in a moderately hot tandoor or over a charcoal grill for 3-4 minutes. In the pre-heated oven, for 4-5 minutes.

TO SERVE

Place three potatoes on each of four individual potatoes and serve with a salad.

———————— • ————————

JHANGI CHAAMPAAN

INGREDIENTS

The Chops

8 *Chaamp*/Kid/Lamb Chops (3-rib)
30g/5 tsp Garlic Paste (strain)
20g/3¼ tsp Ginger Paste (strain)
25g/2 Tbs *Desi Ghee*/Clarified Butter
5 *Chotti Elaichi*/Green Cardamom

3 *Lavang*/Cloves
2 sticks *Daalcheeni*/Cinnamon (1")
150g/5 oz *Dahi*/Yoghurt (whisk)
Salt

The Kheema

400g/14 oz *Kheema*/Kid/Lamb Mince
75ml/6 Tbs *Desi Ghee*/Clarified Butter
4 flakes Garlic (chop)
100g/3 oz Onions (chop)
10g/1" piece Ginger (chop)
4 Green Chillies (seed & chop)
4.5g/1½ tsp Red Chilli Powder
4 Tomatoes (large; chop)
4.5g/1½tsp *Jeera*/Cumin Powder
1.5g/½ tsp *Motti Elaichi*/
   Black Cardamom Powder

0.75g/¼ tsp *Lavang*/Clove Powder
0.75g/¼ tsp *Maghay* Powder
   (or *Daalcheeni*/Cinnamon Powder)
A generous pinch of *Kasoori Methi*/
   Dried Fenugreek Leaf Powder
30ml/2 Tbs Lemon Juice
10g/3 Tbs *Taaza Dhania*/Coriander (chop)
Ginger julienne pickled in lemon juice
Salt

Serves: 4
Preparation Time: 1:15 hours
Cooking Time: 25-30 minutes

PREPARATION

THE CHOPS: Mix all the ingredients in a *handi*/pan, evenly rub the meat with this marinade and reserve for at least 2 hours. Transfer *handi*/pan to heat; add 240ml/1 cup of water and *bhunno*/stir-fry over medium heat. When the juices begin to boil, reduce to low heat and *bhunno*/stir-fry until the meat is cooked and the juices have evaporated. Remove and keep aside. (Add small quantities of water if necessary to prevent sticking.)

COOKING

Spread ghee on a *tawa*/griddle, add garlic, sauté over medium heat with a spatula until light golden, add onions and sauté until onions become translucent and glossy. Add ginger and green chillies, and stir for a few seconds. Then add mince and red chillies, *bhunno*/stir-fry until the chops are cooked (add small quantities of water, as and when necessary, to prevent sticking), add tomatoes and *bhunno*/stir-fry until the fat leaves the sides. Now add the cooked chops and *bhunno*/stir-fry until the mince nappes the meat. Sprinkle cumin, cardamom, clove and maghay (or cinnamon) powders, stir, add kasoori methi salt, and stir. Now add lemon juice, turn with a spatula to incorporate, add coriander and stir, turning with the spatula to incorporate. Remove and adjust the seasoning.

TO SERVE

Remove to a platter and serve with Phulka, Pao or Chappati.

LAWRENCE ROAD de TAWE de TIKKA TAKA TIN

INGREDIENTS

The Tikka

1.2 Kg/2¼ lb *Dasti*/Shoulder of Kid/
    Lamb (boned; ¾" cubes)
25g/2 Tbs *Desi Ghee*/Clarified Butter
6 *Chotti Elaichi*/Green Cardamom
6 *Lavang*/Cloves
3 *Motti Elaichi*/Black Cardamom
3 sticks *Daalcheeni*/Cinnamon (1")

30g/5 tsp Garlic Paste (strain)
20g/3¼ tsp Ginger Paste (strain)
250ml/9 oz *Dahi*/Yoghurt (whisk)
6g/2 tsp Red Chilli Powder
100g/3 oz Fried Onions (crisp brown)
Salt

The Tawa Cooking

100g/½ cup *Desi Ghee*/Clarified Butter
8 flakes Garlic (chop)
200g/7 oz Onions (chop)
15g/1½" piece Ginger (chop)
4 Green Chillies (seed & chop)
3 Tomatoes (large; chop)
4.5g/1½ tsp *Jeera*/Cumin Powder
4.5g/1½ tsp Black Pepper
    (freshly roasted & coarsely ground)

1.5g/½ tsp *Motti Elaichi*/
    Black Cardamom Powder
0.75g/¼ tsp *Lavang*/Clove Powder
0.75g/¼ tsp *Daalcheeni*/Cinnamon (1")
30ml/2 Tbs Dark Rum (XXX)
3g/1tsp *Kasoori Methi*/ Fenugreek Leaves
15ml/1Tbsp Lemon Juice
10g/3 Tbs *Taaza Dhania*/Coriander (chop)
Salt

Serves: 4
Preparation Time: 3:15 hours
Cooking Time: 15 minutes

PREPARATION

THE TIKKA: Mix all the ingredients in a *handi*/pan, evenly rub the meat with this marinade and reserve for at least 2 hours. Transfer *handi*/pan to heat and *bhunno*/stir-fry over medium heat. When the juices begin to boil, reduce to low heat and *bhunno*/stir-fry until the meat is cooked and the juices have evaporated. Remove and keep aside. (Add small quantities of water if necessary to prevent sticking.)

COOKING

Spread ghee on a *tawa*/griddle, add garlic, sauté over medium heat with a spatula until light golden, add onions and sauté until onions become translucent and glossy. Add ginger and green chillies, stir for a few seconds, add tomatoes and *bhunno*/stir-fry until they become soft (release their juices). Then add the cooked meat and *bhunno*/stir-fry until the masala nappes the meat. Sprinkle cumin, pepper, cardamom, clove and cinnamon powders, stir, add salt, and stir. Now add rum, turn with a spatula to incorporate, add coriander, lemon juice, sprinkle kasoori methi and stir, turning with the spatula to incorporate. Remove and adjust the seasoning.

TO SERVE

Remove to flat dish and serve as a cocktail snack, or as a starter, or as an entré with Phulka, Chappati or Tandoori Roti.

TANDOORI JHEENGA

INGREDIENTS

12 Prawns (shell but retain the tails; remove veins)

Desi Ghee/Clarified Butter for basting

The First Marination

60ml/¼ cup White Wine (dry)
60ml/¼ cup Lemon Juice
30g/5 tsp Garlic Paste (strain)

15g/2½ tsp Ginger Paste (strain)
10g/1¾ tsp Green Chilli Paste
Salt

The Second Marination

100g/3 oz Yoghurt Cheese*
60ml/¼ cup Cream
30ml/2 Tbs Lemon Juice
25g/4 tsp Garlic Paste (strain)
15g/2½ tsp Ginger Paste (strain)
Salt

A pinch *Ajwain*/Carom Seeds
3g/1 tsp *Kashmiri Deghi Mirch* Powder
A small pinch *Daalcheeni/*
  Cinnamon Powder
A small pinch *Lavang*/Clove Powder

Serves: 4
Preparation Time: 1:20 hours
Cooking Time: 5-6 minutes

PREPARATION

THE FIRST MARINATION: Mix all the ingredients in a bowl, evenly rub the prawns with this marinade and reserve for 15 minutes. Then squeeze gently between the palms to remove excess moisture.

THE SECOND MARINATION: Put yoghurt cheese in a bowl, add the remaining ingredients and whisk. Evenly rub the prawns with this marinade and reserve in the refrigerator for 1 hour.

THE OVEN· Pre-heat to 350°F.

THE SKEWERING: Skewer the prawns (they should touch without overlapping) and keep a tray underneath to collect the drippings.

* Or what is thick yoghurt, without whey, obtained by hanging curd in muslin cloth to allow the whey to drain out.

COOKING

Roast in a moderately hot tandoor, on a charcoal grill or in a pre-heated oven for 2-3 minutes. Remove, baste with ghee and roast again for 2 minutes.

•

MACHCHI da TIKKA

INGREDIENTS

1kg/2¼ lb Pink Salmon/White Tuna

The First Marination

90ml/6 Tbs Red Wine Vinegar
35g/2 Tbs Garlic Paste (strain)
15g/2½ tsp Ginger Paste (strain)

2.5g/1 tsp Fennel Seeds
1 *Chakriphool*/Star Anise
Salt

The Second Marination

150g/5 oz *Chakka Dahi*/Yoghurt Cheese/
  Hung Yoghurt
30ml/2 Tbs Cream
27.5g/¼ cup Cheddar (grate & mash)
30ml/2 Tbs Mustard Oil
1.25g/½ tsp *Ajwain*/Carom Seeds

2.25g/¾ tsp Paprika Powder
1 sprig Dill (chop)
5g/1 tsp Honey
10ml/2 tsp Lemon Juice
Salt

The Sprinkler

A generous pinch of *Amchoor*/Mango Powder
A generous pinch of Black Rock Salt

A generous pinch of *Kasoori Methi*/
  Fenugreek Leaf Powder

Serves: 4
Preparation Time: 45 minutes
Cooking Time: 4-5 minutes

PREPARATION

THE FISH: Clean, bone, wash, pat dry and cut into 2½" cubes.

THE FIRST MARINATION: Mix all the ingredients, evenly rub the fish cubes with this marinade and reserve for 15 minutes.

THE SECOND MARINATION: Whisk yoghurt cheese in a bowl, add the remaining ingredients, mix well, evenly rub the fish cubes with this marinade and reserve for 15 minutes.

THE SKEWERING: Skewer the cubes slightly apart, keep a tray underneath to collect the drippings.

COOKING

Roast in a moderately hot tandoor for 3-4 minutes, on a charcoal grill, for the same time, in a pre-heated, oven (on a greased baking tray) for 5-6 minutes. Remove and hang the skewers to allow the excess moisture to drip off. Roast again for a minute.

———————— • ————————

AMRITSARI MACHCHI

INGREDIENTS

2 Singhara/Malli/Sole (1 Kg/2¼ lb each)   Mustard Oil to deep fry

The Batter

45g/1½ oz *Besan*/Gramflour   2.5g/1 tsp *Ajwain*/Carom Seeds
30g/5¼ tsp Garlic Paste (strain)   A generous pinch of *Heeng*/Asafoetida
20g/3½ tsp Ginger Paste (strain)   Salt
3g/1 tsp Red Chilli Powder

The Machchi Masala

65g/2¼ oz *Jeera*/Cumin Seeds   5g/1 tsp *Heeng*/Asafoetida
65g/2¼ oz Black Peppercorns   4g/¾ tsp *Tartari*/Tartaric Acid (granules)
60g/2 oz *Kaala Namak*/Black Rock Salt   150g/5¼ oz *Amchoor*/Mango Powder
30g/1 oz *Pudhina*/Dry Mint Leaves   20g/¾ oz *Saunth*/Ginger Powder
5g/2 tsp *Ajwain*/Carom Seeds   20g/¾ oz Yellow Chilli Powder

Serves: 4
Preparation Time: 1 hour
Cooking Time: 15 minutes/set

PREPARATION

THE FISH: Clean, but retain the skin (this is optional if you're squeamish; in any event, it can be discarded at the time of eating), remove the centre bone carefully to obtain two fillets from each fish, trim, wash and pat dry.

THE MARINATION: Put all the ingredients, in a large bowl; add 60ml/¼ cup of water and mix to make a thin batter. Evenly rub the fillets with this batter and reserve in the bowl for 30 minutes.

THE MACHCHI MASALA: Put all ingredients, except mango powder, salt, ginger powder and yellow chilli powder, in mortar and pound with pestle to make fine powder. Transfer to clean, dry bowl, add remaining ingredients and mix well. Sieve and store in sterilized, dry and airtight container. Yield: Approx 450g/1lb.

COOKING

Heat oil in a *kadhai*/wok and deep fry in convenient batches over medium heat until light golden. Remove to absorbent paper to drain excess fat and cool. When cool, make one slit down the middle along the length and 4 slits across the breadth. Then re-heat oil and deep fry fish again until golden and crusty. Remove to absorbent paper to drain excess fat.

TO SERVE

Place a paper doily on a platter; arrange the fillets on top; serve with grated-radish-in-mint-chutney and lemon wedges.

———————— • ————————

TANDOORI BATAER

INGREDIENTS

12 Japanese Quails   Butter for basting

The First Marination

30g/5 tsp Garlic Paste (strain)   60ml/¼ cup *Sirka*/Malt Vinegar
20g/3¼ tsp Ginger Paste (strain)   Salt

The Second Marination

130g/½ cup *Chakka Dahi*/Yoghurt
   Cheese/Hung Yoghurt
55g/½ cup Processed/Cheddar Cheese
2 Raw Mangoes (in summer)
100g/2 cups *Taaza Dhania*/Coriander
35g/1 cup *Taaza Pudhina*/Mint
6 Green Chillies
A generous pinch *Kaala Namak*/
   Black Rock Salt Powder

Salt
3g/1 tsp Black Pepper (freshly roasted &
   coarsely ground)
1.5g/½ tsp *Chotti Elaichi*/
   Green Cardamom Powder
0.75g/¼ tsp *Lavang*/Clove Powder
A pinch of *Javitri*/Mace Powder
20ml/4 tsp Lemon Juice

Serves: 4
Preparation Time: 1: 45 hours
Cooking Time: In Tandoor—7-8 minutes
                On Charcoal Grill—10 minutes
                In Oven—15 minutes

PREPARATION

THE QUAILS: Clean, remove the skin, make slanting incisions—2 on each breast, 2 on each thigh and 1 on each drumstick.

THE FIRST MARINATION: Mix all the ingredients, evenly rub the quails with this marinade and reserve for 15 minutes.

THE SECOND MARINATION: Whisk the yoghurt cheese in a bowl. Grate and then mash the cheese with the base of the palm. Peel, halve, remove the pit and roughly chop raw mangoes. Wash green chillies, slit, seed, roughly cut and discard the stems. Put the raw mangoes, coriander, mint and green chillies in a blender, and make a smooth paste. (To bring out the best flavour, make the paste with a *sil-batta*/stone grinder.) Remove, add yoghurt cheese and the remaining ingredients, and mix well. Evenly rub the quails with this marinade and reserve for 1 hour.

THE SKEWERING: Skewer the quails, from tail to head, touching but not overlapping. Keep a tray underneath to collect the drippings. For the oven, arrange the birds on a greased roasting tray and baste with butter.

THE OVEN: Pre-heat to 375°F.

COOKING

Roast in a moderately hot tandoor for 4 minutes, remove, hang the skewers to allow the excess moisture to drip off, baste with butter and roast again for 2 minutes. Arrange the quails on a pre-heated charcoal grill and roast over medium heat, turning and basting at regular intervals, for 10 minutes. Place the tray in the pre-heated oven and roast, turning and basting with butter and the drippings twice, for 15 minutes or until cooked and coloured.

———————•———————

BHATTI da MURGA PINDIWALA

INGREDIENTS

8 Chicken Legs (with bone)   *Desi Ghee*/Clarified Butter for basting

The Marination

45ml/3 Tbs Cooking Oil
30g/5 tsp Garlic Paste (strain)
20g/3½ tsp Ginger Paste (strain)
45ml/3 Tbs Yoghurt (whisk)
60ml/4 Tbs Malt Vinegar
3g/1 tsp *Jeera*/Cumin Powder
3g/1 tsp *Dhania*/Coriander Powder
3g/1 tsp Black Pepper (freshly roasted & coarsely ground)
3g/1 tsp *Kashmiri Deghi Mirch* Powder

1.5g/½ tsp *Daalcheeni*/Cinnamon Powder
1.5g/½ tsp *Chotti Elaichi*/Green Cardamom Powder
1.5g/½ tsp *Lavang*/Clove Powder
0.75g/¼ tsp *Javitri*/Mace Powder
0.375g/⅛ tsp *Jaiphal*/Nutmeg Powder
0.375g/⅛ tsp *Maghay* Powder
A generous pinch of *Kasoori Methi*/ Dried Fenugreek Leaf Powder
Salt

Serves: 4
Preparation Time: 30 minutes (plus 6 hours marination time)
Cooking Time: 8-10 minutes

PREPARATION

THE CHICKEN: Clean, make angular and deep incision—3 on each thigh and 2 on each drumstick.

THE MARINATION: Heat oil in a *kadhai*/wok, add garlic and ginger, *bhunno*/stir-fry over medium heat until the moisture evaporates. Remove *kadhai*/wok from heat, stir-in yoghurt, mix well, transfer to a large bowl and cool. When cool, mix the remaining ingredients, vigorously rub the chicken legs with this marinade and reserve in the bowl for 6 hours.

COOKING

Place the marinated chicken in convenient batches on a charcoal grill and roast over medium heat for 5-6 minutes, turning once, and basting with ghee at regular intervals. Remove, separate the drumstick bone from thigh bone, without separating the meat. Return chicken to grill and roast for a further 2-3 minutes, turning and basting once.

TO SERVE

Arrange the chicken on a platter and serve as a starter or snack with Mint Chutney and shredded radish and/or onion rings sprinkled with Chaat Masala.

—————————— • ——————————

MURG MALAAI KEBAB

INGREDIENTS

12 Supremes of Chicken

The First Marination

35g/2 Tbs Ginger Paste (strain)
25g/4 tsp Garlic Paste (strain)

60ml/¼ cup *Sirka*/Malt Vinegar
30ml/2 Tbs White Wine

The Second Marination

260g/1 cup *Chakka Dahi*/Yoghurt Cheese (Hung Yoghurt)
60g/2 oz Processed Cheese
1.5g/½ tsp *Dhania*/Coriander Powder
1.5g/½ tsp *Kashmiri Deghi Mirch*
1.5g/½ tsp *Saunf*/Fennel Powder
0.75g/¼ tsp *Chotti Elaichi*/Green Cardamom Powder

0.375g/⅛ tsp *Daalcheeni*/Cinnamon Powder
0.375g/⅛ tsp *Javitri*/Mace Powder
0.375g/⅛ tsp *Jaiphal*/Nutmeg Powder
3.25g/1 Tbs *Taaza Dhania*/Coriander
Salt
120ml/½ cup Cream
0.5g/1 tsp *Zaafraan*/Saffron

Serves: 4
Preparation Time: 1:45 hours
Cooking Time: Upto 15 minutes

PREPARATION

THE CHICKEN: Clean, bone, cut each breast into 3 equal-sized tikka, wash and pat dry.

THE FIRST MARINATION: Mix all the ingredients, rub the chicken pieces with this marinade and reserve for 15 minutes.

THE SECOND MARINATION: Whisk yoghurt cheese in a bowl. Grate processed cheese and mash. Clean, wash and finely chop coriander. Crush saffron threads with a pestle or the back of a spoon, reserve in 15ml/1 Tbs of cream for 15 minutes and then make a paste. Mix cheese, coriander and remaining ingredients with the yoghurt cheese, whisk, stir-in remaining cream, rub the chicken pieces with the marinade and reserve in the refrigerator for 1 hour.

THE SKEWERING: If cooking in the oven, thread three tikka on wooden skewers and keep aside. If cooking in the tandoor or on a charcoal grill skewer the tikka and keep a tray underneath to collect the drippings.

THE OVEN: Pre-heat to 350°F.

COOKING

Roast in a moderately hot tandoor for approximately 8-10 minutes; on a charcoal grill for about the same time, in a pre-heated oven for 14-15 minutes, basting with butter at regular intervals.

MURG TAASH KEBAB

INGREDIENTS

6 Breasts of Chicken (Large)   *Desi Ghee*/Clarified Butter for shallow frying

THE MARINATION

30ml/2Tbsp Lemon Juice
1.5g/2tsp *Daalcheeni*/ Cinnamon Powder
5.6g/1tsp Garlic Paste (strain)

3g/½ tsp Ginger Paste (strain)
2g/½ tsp Black Pepper Powder
Salt

THE FILLING

The 1st Filling

3 Large Tomatoes (cut into roundels)
10g/1½Tbsp Red Chilli Paste

3g/ ½ tsp *Saunf* / Fennel Powder
Salt

The 2nd Filling

1 Large Potato (Peeled and sliced into thin roundels)
2 Onion (Peeled and sliced into thin roundels)
10g/3Tbsp Mint Leaves (chopped)

2 Green Chilli (deseeded and chopped fine)
3g/ ½ tsp Garlic Paste (strain)
1.5g/ ¼ tsp Ginger Paste (strain)
2g/ ½ tsp *Amchoor*/Dried Mango Powder

THE BATTER

130g/ ½ cup *Chakka Dahi*/ Yoghurt Cheese/Hung Yoghurt (whisk)
Salt
3g/1tsp White Pepper Powder

0.375g/¹/₈ tsp *Gulaabpankhrhi*/ Rose Petal Powder
30ml/2 Tbs Cream

Serves: 4
Preparation Time: 2 hours
Cooking Time: 4-5 minutes

PREPARATION

THE CHICKEN: : Clean, bone, wash and pat dry. With a sharp knife, cut each breast into half horizontally.

THE MARINATION: Crush cinnamon. Put lemon juice, ginger, garlic, black pepper powder and salt in a large bowl, mix well, rub the chicken with this marinade and reserve for 45 minutes.

THE 1st FILLING: Mix the fennel powder and salt thoroughly in the chilli paste with a spoon. Arrange the tomato slices on a tray and smear them thoroughly with the paste.

THE 2nd FILLING: Mix all the ingredients together in a bowl and reserve in a refrigerator.

THE BATTER: Mix the dried rose petal powder with cream and slowly whisk in with the yoghurt.

THE ASSEMBLING

Arrange the tomato slices coated with chilli and fennel paste on a slice of chicken breast evenly and cover with another. Place couple of onion and potato slices each over the second slice and place a third roundel on top. Hold these three slices of chicken firmly and dip in the batter. Repeat the procedure with the other slices and arrange on a tray and refrigerate for 10 minutes.

THE SKEWERING: Pierce 2 of chicken tiers and small potatoes (to prevent chicken from touching or sliding down), alternately, in a skewer and keep a tray underneath to collect drippings.

COOKING

Roast in moderately hot tandoor for 5-6 minutes or on charcoal grill for 7-8 minutes, in pre-heated oven (275°F) for 10-11 minutes.

TO SERVE

Unskewer chicken and potatoes (discard), arrange the chicken on a platter and serve hot with mint chutney.

———————————— • ————————————

TANDOORI KUKARH

INGREDIENTS

2 Chicken (600g each)   Butter for basting

The First Marination

20g/3½ Cup Garlic Paste (strained)   60ml Lemon Juice
10g/1¾ Ginger Paste (strained)

The Second Marination

160g/¾ cup Yoghurt   3g *Motti Elaichi*/Black Cardamom Powder
45ml Cream   2g *Chhoti Elaichi*/Green Cardamom Powder
40g/7 tsp Garlic Paste (strained)   2g *Daalcheeni*/Cinnamon Powder
20g/3½ tsp Ginger Paste (strained)   2g *Gulaabpankhrhi*/Rose Petal Powder
3g/1 tsp Red Chilli Powder   0.5g *Zaafraan*/Saffron
3g/1 tsp *Jeera*/Cumin Powder   Salt

Serves: 4
Preparation Time: 4:30 hours
Cooking Time: 15 minutes

PREPARATION

THE CHICKEN: Clean, remove the skin, make deep incision—2 on each breast, 2 on each thigh, 3 on each drumstick.

THE FIRST MARINATION: Mix all the ingredients and rub the chicken evenly with this marinade. Reserve for 20 minutes.

THE SECOND MARINATION: Whisk yoghurt in a large bowl, add the remaining ingredients and mix well. Rub the chicken with this marinade and reserve for 4 hours in the refrigerator.

THE OVEN: Pre-heat to 350° F.

THE SKEWERING: Skewer the chicken, from tail to head. Keep a tray underneath to collect the drippings.

COOKING

Roast in a moderately hot tandoor for approx 8 minutes, on a charcoal grill for about the same time and in the pre-heated oven for 10 minutes or until half cooked. Remove and hang the skewers to allow the excess moisture to drip off (approx. 4-5 minutes), baste with butter and roast again for 3-4 minutes.

———————— • ————————

TANDOORI CHOOZA

INGREDIENTS

12 Thighs of Chicken

The First Marination

35g/2 Tbs Garlic Paste (strain)
25g/4 tsp Ginger Paste (strain)
10g/1¾ tsp Green Chilli Paste

60ml/¼ cup *Sirka*/Malt Vinegar
Salt

The Second Marination

260g/1 cup *Chakka Dahi*/Yoghurt Cheese/
   Hung Yoghurt
55g/½ cup Processed Cheese
45g/7¾ tsp Raw Mango Paste
3g/1 tsp *Kashmiri Deghi Mirch* Powder
3g/1 tsp *Jeera*/Cumin Powder

1.5g/½ tsp *Dhania*/Coriander Powder
1.5g/¼ tsp *Chotti Elaichi*/
   Green Cardamom Powder
3.25g/1 Tbs *Taaza Dhania*/Coriander
Salt
120ml/½ cup Cream

Serves: 4
Preparation Time: 1:45 hours
Cooking Time: Up to 10 minutes

PREPARATION

THE CHICKEN: Clean, bone, cut each thigh into 2 equal-sized tikka, wash and pat dry.

THE FIRST MARINATION: Mix all the ingredients, rub the chicken pieces with this marinade and reserve for 15 minutes.

THE SECOND MARINATION: Whisk yoghurt cheese in a bowl. Grate processed cheese and mash with the base of the palm. Clean, wash and finely chop coriander. Mix cheese, coriander and remaining ingredients with the yoghurt cheese, whisk, stir-in remaining cream, rub the tikka with the marinade and reserve in the refrigerator for 1 hour.

THE SKEWERING: If cooking in the oven, thread three tikka on wooden skewers and keep aside. If cooking in the tandoor or on a charcoal grill skewer the tikka and keep a tray underneath to collect the drippings.

THE OVEN: Pre-heat to 350°F.

COOKING

Roast in a moderately hot tandoor for approximately 6-7 minutes. On a charcoal grill for about the same time. In a pre-heated oven for 8-10 minutes, basting with butter at regular intervals.

KUKARH da PAKORHA

INGREDIENTS

16 *Tangrhi*/Chicken Drumsticks
   (large & juicy)
Sarson/Mustard Oil to deep fry
60g/2 oz *Maida*/Flour
60g/2 oz *Besan*/Gramflour
30g/1 oz *Arraroot*/Cornflour
2 Eggs
20g/3¼ tsp Garlic Paste (strain)
15g/2½ tsp Ginger Paste (strain)
1g/½ tsp *Ajwain*/Carom Seeds
3g/1 tsp *Kashmiri Deghi Mirch* Powder
4.5g/1½ tsp *Jeera*/Cumin Powder
1.5g/½ tsp *Motti Elaichi*/
   Black Cardamom Powder

0.75g/¼ tsp *Lavang*/Clove Powder
0.75g/¼ tsp *Maghay* Powder
   (or *Daalcheeni*/Cinnamon Powder)
0.375g/⅛ tsp *Jaiphal*/Nutmeg Powder
10g/1Tbsp *Dhania*/Coriander Seeds
   (freshly roasted and coarsely ground)
0.6g/1tsp Black Pepper (freshly roasted &
   coarsely ground)
Salt
2 Green Chillies (seed & chop)
10ml/2 tsp Lemon Juice

Serves: 4
Preparation Time: 3:15 hours
Cooking Time: 4-5 minutes per set

PREPARATION

THE BATTER: Beat eggs in a bowl; add the remaining ingredients and enough water to make a batter of fritter (pakorha) consistency.

COOKING

Heat oil in a *kadhai*/wok to a smoking point over medium heat, remove and cool. Re-heat oil; add a few drops of the batter; as soon as the batter droplets come to the surface, dip the chicken drumsticks in the batter and deep fry until crisp and golden. Remove to absorbent paper to drain the excess fat.

TO SERVE

Arrange doily paper on a service platter, place the pakorha on top and serve with Mint Chutney.

MASALEDAAR CHAAMPAAN

INGREDIENTS

1.2Kg/ 2²/₃ lb Lamb Chops
175g/1 cup Onions
120g/ ½ cup Tomatoes
30g/5tsp Ginger Paste
50g/3Tbsp Garlic Paste

225g/1 cup Yoghurt
Salt
5g/1tsp Red Chilli Powder
6g/2tsp *Jeera*/Cumin Seeds
5g/1tsp *Garam Masala*

The Garnish

20g/2Tbsp Ginger

15ml/1Tbsp Lemon Juice

Serves: 4
Preparation Time: 25 minutes
Cooking Time: 1:10 minutes

PREPARATION

THE LAMB: Clean and make 2 rib chops.

THE VEGETABLES: Peel, wash and roughly chop onions. Wash and roughly chop tomatoes.

THE YOGHURT: Whisk in a bowl.

THE CUMIN: Broil, put in a blender and make a fine powder.

THE GARNISH: Scrape, wash and cut ginger into fine juliennes and immediately marinate in lemon juice until the chops are ready to be served.

COOKING

Put all the ingredients, except cumin, garam masala and the garnish, in a *kadhai*/wok, bring to a boil, cover and simmer until chops are tender. Remove the chops and keep aside. *Bhunno*/stir-fry the masala until half the liquid has evaporated. Add cumin, stir for a minute, return the chops to the *kadhai*/wok and simmer for 3 minutes. Sprinkle garam masala and stir. Adjust the seasoning.

TO SERVE

Arrange the lamb chops on a flat dish, spread the masala on top, garnish with the marinated ginger juliennes and serve with Phulka or Tandoori Roti.

BALUCHI TIKKA

INGREDIENTS

1Kg/2¼ lb Shoulder of Kid/Lamb (½" cubes)

1st Marination

15g/2½ tsp Garlic Paste

6g/1tsp Ginger Paste

60ml/ ¼ cup Malt Vinegar

6g/2tsp Red Chilli Powder

2nd Marination

100g/3 oz Yoghurt Cheese

45g/7¾ tsp Raw Papaya Paste

30g/5 tsp Garlic Paste (strain)

20g/3¼ tsp Ginger Paste (strain)

60ml/¼ cup Sherry

45ml/3 Tbs Malt Vinegar

30ml/2 Tbs Cream

1.25g/½ tsp *Shahi Jeera*/Black
    Cumin Seeds

3g/1 tsp Black Pepper (freshly roasted &
    coarsely ground)

1.5g/½ tsp *Jeera*/Cumin Powder

1.5g/½ tsp Red Chilli Powder

0.75g /¼ tsp *Motti Elaichi*/
    Black Cardamom Powder

0.75g/¼ tsp *Chotti Elaichi*/
    Green Cardamom Powder

0.375g/⅛ tsp *Daalcheeni*/
    Cinnamon Powder

0.375g/⅛ tsp *Lavang*/Clove Powder

A pinch of *Jaiphal*/Nutmeg Powder

A pinch of *Javitri*/Mace Powder

A pinch of *Gulaabpankhrhi*/
    Rose Petal Powder

A pinch of *Kaala Namak*/
    Black Rock Salt Powder

Salt

Serves: 4

Preparation Time: 2:30 hours(3 hours for 1st marination)

Cooking Time: 10-12 minutes

PREPARATION

THE 1st MARINATION: Mix all the ingredients together and rub into the cubes of lamb. reserve in a refrigerator for three hours.

THE 2nd MARINATION : Whisk yoghurt cheese in a large bowl, add the remaining ingredients, mix well, rub the cubes evenly with this marinade and reserve for 2 hours.

THE SKEWERING: Skewer the cubes and keep a tray underneath to collect the drippings.

COOKING

Roast on a moderately hot charcoal grill for 5-6 minutes. Remove the skewers and allow the excess moisture to drip off (approx 2-3 minutes), baste with butter and roast again for 2-3 minutes.

———————— • ————————

RAAN PESHAWRI

INGREDIENTS

2 Leg of Kid/Lamb (approx 3 lb/1.3 Kg)
5 *Chotti Elaichi*/Green Cardamom
3 *Motti Elaichi*/Black Cardamom
3 *Lavang*/Cloves

2 *Tej Patta*/Bay Leaf
2 sticks *Daalcheeni*/Cinnamon (1")
Butter to baste

The 1st Marination

Salt
12g/4 tsp Red Chilli Powder
40g/7 tsp Garlic Paste (strain)

20g/3½ tsp Ginger Paste (strain)
60ml/¼ cup *Sirka*/Malt Vinegar
45g/1½ oz Raw Papaya Paste

The 2nd Marination

100g/3 oz Yoghurt
30g/5 tsp Garlic Paste (strain)
20g/3¼ tsp Ginger Paste (strain)
30ml/2 Tbs Cream
1.25g/½ tsp *Shahi Jeera*/
  Black Cumin Seeds
3g/1 tsp Black Pepper (freshly roasted &
  coarsely ground)
1.5g/½ tsp *Jeera*/Cumin Powder

0.75g/¼ tsp *Chotti Elaichi*/
  Green Cardamom Powder
0.375g/⅛ tsp *Daalcheeni*/
  Cinnamon Powder
0.375g/⅛ tsp *Lavang*/Clove Powder
A pinch of *Jaiphal*/Nutmeg Powder
A pinch of *Javitri*/Mace Powder
A pinch of *Gulaabpankhrhi*/
  Rose Petal Powder

1.5g/½ tsp Red Chilli Powder
0.75g/¼ tsp *Motti Elaichi*/
   Black Cardamom Powder

A pinch of *Kaala Namak*/
   Black Rock Salt Powder
Salt

Serves: 4
Preparation: 4:30 hours
Cooking: 16-20 minutes

PREPARATION

THE KID/LAMB LEG: Clean, remove the blade bone and then, using boning knife, loosen meat around thighbone (do not expose bone, merely loosen meat). Wash and pat dry.

THE MARINATION

1st Marination

Forcefully rub, as in massage, kid/lamb leg, inside and out, with salt. Repeat process with red chillies, garlic paste, ginger paste and vinegar. (Remember, each of these ingredients is to be rubbed separately and not as mixture). Refrigerate for 2 hours.

2nd Marination

Whisk the yoghurt in a bowl; mix all the ingredients in it. Pour this marinade over the lamb legs, rub thoroughly and refrigerate for 2 hours.

THE OVEN: Pre-heat to 350°F.

THE BRAISING: Arrange kid/lamb leg in roasting pan (pan should be just about large enough for leg), add green and black cardamom, cloves, bay leaves, cinnamon and just enough water to cover legs. Then cover pan loosely with lid or foil (it shouldn't be sealed or air-tight), braise in pre-heated oven for an hour, reduce oven temperature (to 275°F) and continue to braise until meat is tender and leaves bones from ends, and the liquor is almost absorbed.

SKEWERING: Skewer right down middle, horizontally, and as close to bone as possible. For the oven, arrange the legs on a greased roasting tray and baste with butter.

COOKING

Roast in a moderately hot tandoor for 4 minutes, remove, hang the skewers to allow the excess moisture to drip off, baste with butter and roast again for 2 minutes. Arrange the legs on a pre-heated charcoal grill and roast over medium heat, turning and basting at regular intervals, for 6-7 minutes. Place the tray in the pre-heated oven and roast, turning and basting with butter and the drippings twice, for 6-7 minutes or until cooked and coloured.

———————— • ————————

SEEKH LAHORI

INGREDIENTS

800g/1lb 13 oz *Kheema*/Kid/Lamb Mince (with 10% kid/lamb fat)
30g/1 oz Onions (finely chop)
15g/1½" piece Ginger (finely chop)
8 flakes Garlic (finely chop)
4 Green Chillies (seed & finely chop)
10g/3 Tbs *Taaza Dhania*/Coriander (chop)
2 Eggs
60g/2 oz Cheese (grate)
3g/1 tsp *Anaardaana*/Pomegranate Powder
3g/1 tsp Black Pepper (freshly roasted & coarsely ground)
1.5g/½ tsp *Pudhina*/Mint Powder

0.75g/¼ tsp *Chotti Elaichi*/ Green Cardamom Powder
0.375g/⅛ tsp *Motti Elaichi*/ Black Cardamom Powder
0.375g/⅛ tsp *Daalcheeni*/ Cinnamon Powder
0.375g/⅛ tsp *Lavang*/Clove Powder
0.375g/⅛ tsp *Jaiphal*/Nutmeg Powder
A generous pinch of *Kaala Namak*/ Black Rock Salt Powder
Salt
Desi Ghee/Clarified Butter for basting

Serves: 4
Preparation Time: 1 hour
Cooking Time: 4-5 minutes

PREPARATION

THE SEEKH MIXTURE: Mix all the ingredients, except ghee, divide into 16 equal portions, make balls and refrigerate for 15 minutes.

THE SKEWERING: Using a moist hand, spread the balls by pressing each along the length of the skewers, 2 inches apart, and making each kebab 6" long.

COOKING

Roast in a moderately hot tandoor for 4 minutes or on a charcoal grill, for about the same time, turning at regular intervals. Remove, baste with ghee and roast again for a minute. The kebab can also be shallow-fried on a *tawa*/griddle, in which case you make croquets and don't skewer the mixture.

TO SERVE

Unskewer, arrange kebab on a platter, sprinkle the masala on top and serve hot with Mint Chutney or Saunth.

BHARWAAN GUCHCHI KANDAHARI

INGREDIENTS

16/24 *Guchchi*/Morels (large/medium)

The Filling

30g/1 oz Fresh Pomegranate

30g/1 oz Yellow Zucchini (remove seeds & cut into brunnoise)

30g/1 oz Carrots (cut into brunnoise)

30g/1 oz *Chakka Dahi*/Yoghurt Cheese/ Hung Yoghurt

5g/½" piece Ginger (finely chop)

2 Green Chillies (seed & finely chop)

3.25g/1 Tbs *Taaza Dhania*/ Coriander (finely chop)

Salt

The Gravy

50g/¼ cup *Desi Ghee*/Clarified Butter

200g/7 oz Boiled Onion Paste

30g/5 tsp Ginger Paste (strain)

150ml/5 oz *Dahi*/Yoghurt

3g/1 tsp *Dhania*/Coriander Powder

3g/1 tsp *Kashmiri Deghi Mirch* Powder

1.5g/½ tsp *Haldee*/Turmeric Powder

30g/1 oz *Kharbooja*/Melon Seed Paste

1 litre/4¼ cups Clear Vegetable Stock or Water

Salt

30ml/2 Tbs Cream

The Garnish

0.25g/¼ tsp *Zaafraan*/Saffron

Toasted Almond Flakes

Serves: 4
Preparation Time: 1 hour
Cooking Time: 30 minutes

PREPARATION

THE MORELS: Soak in hot water for 10 minutes, drain, carefully wash in running water to remove grit and soak again in hot water for 5 minutes or until they become soft and swollen. Drain, carefully squeeze out the excess water and remove the stems to create pockets for the stuffing.

THE FILLING: Put all the ingredients in a bowl, mix well and divide into 16/24 equal portions.

THE STUFFING: Carefully prise open the morels and pack each with a portion of the filling.

THE YOGHURT MIXTURE: Put yoghurt in a bowl, add coriander, deghi mirch and turmeric powders, and whisk to mix well.

THE GARNISH: Reserve saffron threads in 15ml/1 Tbs of lukewarm water.

COOKING

Melt ghee in a *handi*/pan, add onion and ginger pastes, sauté until fat begins to leave the sides (ensure that the masala does not get coloured). Remove *handi*/pan from heat, stir in the yoghurt mixture, return *handi*/pan to heat and *bhunno*/stir-fry until specks of fat begin to appear on the surface. Then add melon seed paste, *bhunno*/stir-fry until specks of fat begin to appear on the surface, add stock (or water), stir, sprinkle salt, stir, bring to a boil, reduce to low heat and simmer, stirring occasionally, until reduced by a third. Now add the stuffed morels, bring to a boil, reduce to low heat and simmer, stirring occasionally, for 2-3 minutes. Remove *handi*/pan from heat, stir-in cream and adjust the seasoning.

TO SERVE

Remove to a service dish, garnish with saffron threads and toasted almond flakes. Serve with Tandoori Paratha or Roti or even Steamed Rice.

———————— • ————————

RANJIT SHAHI PANEER

INGREDIENTS

600g/1lb 5 oz *Paneer*

THE GRAVY

200g/1 cup Butter
30g/5tsp Ginger Paste (strained)
30g/5tsp Garlic Paste (strained)
1 Kg/2lb 4oz Tomatoes
10g/1Tbsp Cinger
4 Green Chillies

20g/1½ Tbsp *Khoya* (grated)
30g/2Tbsp Cashew nut Paste
3g1tsp *Kashmiri Deghi Mirch* Powder
100ml/½ cup Cream
10g/5 Tbsp *Taaza Dhania*/Coriander

THE BHURJEE

200g/7 oz *Paneer* (grated coarse)
120g/1 cup Onions (chopped fine)
150g/ ¾th cup Tomato (chopped)
10g/1¾ tsp Garlic (chopped fine)
6g/1tsp Ginger (chopped fine)
3g/1 tsp *Jeera*/ Cumin Seeds
2g/1tsp Red Chilli Powder
1.5g/½ tsp Black Pepper
  (freshly roasted & coarsely ground)

0.75g/¼ tsp *Daalcheeni*/Cinnamon Powder
0.75g/¼ tsp *Lavang*/Clove Powder
A generous pinch of *Kasoori Methi*/
  Dried Fenugreek Leaf Powder
15ml/1 Tbs Lemon Juice
2 Green Chillies (seed & cut into juliennes)
3.25g/1 Tbs *Taaza Dhania*/Coriander (chop)
Salt

Serves: 4
Preparation Time: 20 minutes
Cooking Time: 40 minutes

PREPARATION

THE PANEER: Cut into 1-inch cubes.

THE VEGETABLES: Remove eyes, wash and roughly chop tomatoes. Scrape, wash and finely chop ginger. Remove stems, wash, slit and deseed green chillies. Clean, wash and chop coriander. Peel and chop onion fine.

COOKING

Melt half the butter in a *handi*/pan, add the ginger and garlic pastes, stir over medium heat until the moisture evaporates, add tomatoes and water (approx 500 ml), stir for a minute, reduce to low heat, cover and simmer, stirring occasionally, until tomatoes are mashed. Remove and pass through a fine mesh soup strainer into a separate *handi*/pan. Keep aside.

Melt the remaining butter in a *kadhai*/wok, add the chopped ginger and green chillies, sauté over medium heat for a minute, add khoya, cashewnut paste and *bhunno*/stir-fry until light brown. Then add Kashmiri deghi mirch—the deghi provides excellent colouring—and stir. Now add the strained tomato gravy, bring to a boil, add the paneer cubes and salt, stir, reduce to low heat and simmer for 5-6 minutes. Remove, stir-in cream and adjust the seasoning.

The Bhurjee

Heat ghee in a *kadhai*/wok, add cumin and stir over medium heat until it begins to pop, add onions, sauté until light golden, add the ginger and garlic pastes, *bhunno*/stir-fry until the moisture evaporates. Then add red chilli powder and *bhunno*/stir-fry until the moisture evaporates. Add tomatoes, *bhunno*/stir-fry until the moisture evaporates and the fat leaves the sides. Now add paneer, stir, add green chillies and salt, *bhunno*/stir-fry for a minute, add pepper, clove, cinnamon and kasoori methi, stir, remove and adjust the seasoning.

TO SERVE

Remove to a bowl, garnish with coriander and serve with Tandoori Roti, Naan or Steamed Rice.

———— • ————

KADHAI PANEER

INGREDIENTS

The Paneer

800g/1 lb 13 oz Paneer (2" x ½" x ½" batons)
37.5g/3 Tbs *Desi Ghee*/Clarified Butter
90g/3 oz Onions (chop)
20g/3½ tsp Garlic Paste (strain)
10g/1¾ tsp Ginger Paste (strain)
2g/1 tsp *Dhania*/Coriander Seeds (roast & pound to split)
3g/1 tsp Black Pepper (freshly roasted & coarsely ground)
3g/1 tsp Red Chilli Powder
1.5g/½ tsp *Haldee*/Turmeric Powder
360ml/1½ cups Tomato Purée (canned)
Salt
1 *Harri Shimla Mirch*/Green Bell Pepper (⅛" thick strips)

1 *Peeli Shimla Mirch*/Yellow Bell Pepper (⅛" thick strips)
1 *Laal Shimla Mirch*/Red Bell Peppers (⅛" thick strips)
2.25g/¾ tsp *Jeera*/Cumin Powder
1.5g/½ tsp *Chotti Elaichi*/ Green Cardamom Powder
0.375g/⅛ tsp *Javitri*/Mace Powder
0.375g/⅛ tsp *Daalcheeni*/ Cinnamon Powder
0.375g/⅛ tsp *Lavang*/Clove Powder
A generous pinch of *Kasoori Methi*/ Dried *Methidaana*/Fenugreek Seeds
3.25g/1 Tbs *Taaza Dhania*/Coriander

Serves: 4
Preparation Time: 45 minutes
Cooking Time: 7-8 minutes

COOKING

Heat ghee in a *kadhai*/pan, add onions and sauté until translucent and glossy, add garlic and ginger pastes, and *bhunno*/stir-fry until the moisture evaporates. Add coriander seeds and pepper, *bhunno*/stir-fry until the coriander begins to change colour, add red chillies and turmeric (dissolved in 30ml/2 Tbs of water), and *bhunno*/stir-fry until the moisture evaporates. Then add tomato purée and salt, *bhunno*/stir-fry until specks of fat begin to appear on the surface, add paneer, stir for a minute, add the bell peppers and stir for a minute. Sprinkle the cumin, cardamom, mace, cinnamon, clove and kasoori methi powders, stir carefully, remove and adjust the seasoning.

TO SERVE

Remove to a serving dish, garnish with coriander and serve with Tandoori Roti or Phulka.

———————— • ————————

SARSON da SAAG

INGREDIENTS

750g/1lb 11 oz *Sarson da Saag*/
  Mustard Leaf (roughly chop)
250g/9 oz Spinach (roughly chop)
100g/3 oz *Moolipatta*/White Radish Leaf
  (roughly chop)
30g/1 oz *Bathua* (roughly chop)
30g/3 piece Ginger (dice)

8 Green Chilli (slit & seed)
45g/1½ oz Rice
60ml/¼ cup *Sarson*/Mustard Oil
Salt
15g/½ oz *Makki ka Atta*/Maize flour
200g/1 cup White Butter

Serves: 4
Preparation Time: 30 minutes
Cooking Time: 3 hours

COOKING

Put all the ingredients, except maize flour and white butter, in a *handi*/pan, add water 2 litres/8⅓ cups of water, bring to a boil, reduce to low heat and simmer until the greens are tender (approx 1:45 hours). Remove *handi*/pan from heat and churn with a *madhani* (wooden churner with which *lussee* is churned). Return *handi*/pan to heat, add maize flour, cover and simmer over very low heat, stirring at regular intervals, for one hour. Remove and adjust the seasoning.

TO SERVE

Remove to a bowl, garnish with large dollops of butter and serve with Makki ki Roti.

———————— • ————————

SAAG PANEER

INGREDIENTS

600g/1lb 5½ oz *Paneer*/Cottage Cheese
  (cut into 1½" cubes)
650g/1lb 9 oz Spinach (chop)
150g/5 oz *Methi*/Fresh Fenugreek (chop)
100g/½ cup *Desi Ghee*/Clarified Butter
5 *Chotti Elaichi*/Green Cardamom
4 *Lavang*/Cloves
3 *Motti Elaichi*/Black Cardamom
2 sticks *Daalcheeni*/Cinnamon (1")
2 *Tej Patta*/Bay Leaf
300g/11 oz Onions (chop)
12 flakes Garlic (chop)
15g/1½" piece Ginger (chop)

4 Green Chillies (seed and chop)
3g/1 tsp Red Chilli Powder
3g/1 tsp *Haldee*/Turmeric Powder
Salt
150g/5 oz Tomato (chop)
30ml/2 Tbsp Cream
4.5g/1½ tsp *Jeera*/Cumin Powder
  (freshly roasted)
A generous pinch *Kasoori Methi*/
  Fenugreek Powder
10g/1" piece Ginger (juliennes; reserved
  in 15ml/1 Tbs Lemon Juice)

Serves: 4
Preparation Time: 45 minutes
Cooking Time: 30 minutes

COOKING

Heat ghee in a *kadhai*/wok, add green cardamom, cloves, black cardamom, cinnamon and bay leaf, and stir over medium heat until the green cardamom begins to change colour. Add onions, garlic and sauté until onions are light golden, add ginger and green chillies, stir for a few seconds. Reduce to medium heat, add red chillies, turmeric and salt, and stir for a few seconds. Reduce to low heat, cover and simmer. Add tomatoes and *bhunno*/stir-fry until fat leaves the sides. Now add spinach and fresh fenugreek, and *bhunno*/stir-fry until the liquid has evaporated. Add the paneer cubes and simmer till the spinach and fenugreek nappe the paneer. Finish with cream, cumin and kasoori methi, stir, remove and adjust the seasoning.

TO SERVE

Remove to a service dish, garnish with ginger juliennes and serve with Phulka, Roomali Roti or Tandoori Roti.

PANEER te MUTTAR di BHURJEE

INGREDIENTS

300g/11 oz Green Peas (boil until al dente)
450g/1 lb *Paneer* (mash)
50g/¼ cup *Desi Ghee*/Clarified Butter
2g/1 tsp *Jeera*/Cumin Seeds
90g/3 oz Onions (chop)
10g/1 ¾ tsp Ginger Paste (strain)
20g/3¼ tsp Garlic Paste (strain)
3g/1 tsp *Kashmiri Deghi Mirch* Powder
1.5g/½ tsp *Haldee*/Turmeric Powder
175g/1 cup Tomatoes (chop)
4 Green Chillies (seed & cut into ⅛" thick strips)

Salt
3g/2Tbs *Kasoori Methi*/ Dried Fenugreek Leaves
3g/1 tsp Black Pepper Powder (coarsely ground)
A generous pinch *Chotti Elaichi*/ Green Cardamom Powder
A generous pinch *Lavang*/Clove Powder
15g/1½" piece Ginger (juliennes)
12.5g/¼ cup Coriander (finely chop)

Serves: 4
Preparation Time: 30 minutes
Cooking Time: 15 minutes

COOKING

Heat ghee in a *kadhai*/wok, add cumin and stir over medium heat until it begins to pop, add onions, sauté until light golden, add the ginger and garlic pastes, *bhunno*/stir-fry until the moisture evaporates. Then add red chillies and turmeric (dissolved in 30ml/12 Tbs of water), and *bhunno*/stir-fry until the moisture evaporates. Add tomatoes, *bhunno*/stir-fry until the moisture evaporates, add peas until the fat leaves the sides. Now add paneer, stir, add green chillies and salt, *bhunno*/stir-fry for a minute, add pepper, green cardamom, clove, and kasoori methi, stir, remove and adjust the seasoning.

Bharwaan Guchchi Kandahari (*Exotica*)

Seekh Lahori (*Kebab*)

Kadhai Paneer (*Stir-fry*)

Sarson da Saag (*Popular traditional fare*)

Paneer te Muttar di Bhurjee (*Stir-fry*)

Teekha Paneer Gobhi aur Badaam (*Stir-fry*)

Aloobukhara Kofta (*Veg. Curry*)

TO SERVE

Remove to a flat dish, garnish with ginger and coriander, and serve with Phulka.

———————————— • ————————————

TEEKHA PANEER GOBHI AUR BADAAM

INGREDIENTS

24 batons *Paneer* (1½" x 5/8" x 5/8")
Cooking Oil to deep fry *Paneer*
450g/1 lb Broccoli (medium florets, blanch)
37.5g/3 Tbs *Desi Ghee*/Clarified Butter
45g/1½ oz Onions (chop)
20g/3½ tsp Garlic Paste (strain)
10g/1¾ tsp Ginger Paste (strain)
3g/1 tsp Black Pepper (freshly roasted & coarsely ground)
240ml/1 cups Tomato Purée (canned)
4.5g/1½ tsp *Dhania*/Coriander Powder

Salt
1.5g/½tsp *Chotti Elaichi*/ Green Cardamom Powder
0.375g/⅛ tsp *Jaiphal*/Nutmeg Powder
0.375g/⅛ tsp *Lavang*/Clove Powder
A generous pinch of *Kasoori Methi*/ Dried Fenugreek Leaves
2.5g/1 Tbs *Taaza Pudhina*/ Mint Leaf
15g/½ Toasted Almond Flakes

The Batter

45g/1½ oz Rice Flour
30g/1 oz *Besan*/Gramflour
20g/3¼ tsp *Kari Patta*/Curry Leaf Paste
15g/5 tsp *Dhania*/Coriander Powder
4.5g/1½ tsp Red Chilli Powder

1.5g/½ tsp *Daalcheeni*/Cinnamon Powder
0.75g/¼ tsp *Kebab Cheeni*/Allspice Powder
A generous pinch of *Heeng*/Asafoetida (reserve in 60ml/¼ cup of water)

Serves: 4
Preparation Time: 45 minutes
Cooking Time: 7-8

PREPARATION

THE BATTER : Sift rice and gramflour into a bowl, add the remaining ingredients and mix well. Pour this "batter" on the paneer and mix well.

THE TOMATO PURÉE MIXTURE: Put in a bowl, add coriander powder and salt, and mix well.

COOKING

Heat ghee in a *kadhai*/pan, add onions and sauté until translucent and glossy, add garlic and ginger pastes, and *bhunno*/stir-fry until the moisture evaporates. Add pepper, *bhunno*/stir-fry for a few seconds, add the tomato purée mixture and *bhunno*/stir-fry until specks of fat begin to appear on the surface. Then add broccoli, *bhunno*/stir-fry for a minute, add cardamom, nutmeg, clove and kasoori methi powders, stir for a few seconds, add mint and stir to mix well. Remove and adjust the seasoning. Keep warm.

Heat oil in a *kadhai*/wok, add paneer pieces in convenient batches and deep fry over high heat for 2 minutes. Remove and keep on a *pauni*/perforated spoon for 2 minutes and refry over medium heat for 2 minutes or until the "batter" is crisp. Remove to absorbent paper to drain the excess fat.

TO SERVE

Make a bed of broccoli, arrange paneer on top, garnish with almond flakes and serve.

DHINGRI KOFTA

INGREDIENTS

The Kofta

750g/1 lb 11 oz Spinach
  (remove stems and finely chop)
350g/13 oz Paneer (grate and mash
  with the base of palm)
30ml/2 Tbs Cooking Oil
2g/1 tsp Cumin Seeds

6 flakes Garlic (finely chop)
1.5g/½ tsp White Pepper Powder
Salt
12.5g/2 Tbs Cornflour
Cooking Oil to deep fry kofta

The Filling

8 Morrels (large)
60g/2 oz Oyster Mushrooms

10g/1" piece Ginger (finely chop)
2 Green Chillies (seed & finely chop)

60g/2 oz Button Mushrooms
20g/4 tsp Sugar
30ml/2 Tbs Lemon Juice
12.5g/1 Tbs Butter

3.25g/1 Tbs Sage (dried)
3g/1 tsp Black Pepper Powder
   (coarsely ground)
Salt

The Gravy

50/¼ cup Clarified Butter
20g/3½ tsp Garlic Paste (strain)
20g3½ tsp Ginger Paste (strain)
480ml/2 cups Fresh Tomato Purée
3g/1 tsp Red Chilli Powder
30g/3 Tbs Cashew Nut Paste
1.5g/½ tsp Green Cardamom Powder
0.375g/⅛ tsp Black Cardamom Powder

0.375g/⅛ tsp *Lavang*/Clove Powder
0.375g/⅛ tsp *Dalcheeni*/Cinnamon Powder
0.375g/⅛ tsp *Javitri*/Mace Powder
Salt
A generous pinch crushed *Kasoori Methi*/
   Dried Fenugreek Leaves
60ml/¼ cup Cream

The Garnish

12 Almonds (powder)

30ml/2 Tbs Cream

Serves: 4
Preparation Time: 2:15 hours
Cooking Time: 25 minutes

PREPARATION

THE SPINACH-PANEER MIXTURE: Heat oil in a *kadhai*/wok, add cumin seeds, stir over medium heat until they begin to pop, add garlic, sauté until golden, add spinach and *bhunno/* stir-fry until the moisture has completely evaporated. Remove to a *paraat* and cool. When cool, add the remaining ingredients, mix well, divide into 12 equal portions and keep aside.

THE FILLING: Wash morels in running water to remove grit, drain, soak in lukewarm water for 15 minutes, drain, remove stems, and chop. Remove the earthy base of the oyster and button mushrooms' stalks, wash in running water to remove grit, drain and chop. Put brown sugar and lemon juice in a frying pan and obtain a syrup of one-string consistency over very low heat (ensure that the mixture does not become hard). Then add the mushrooms, cook until the moisture has almost evaporated, add ginger and green chillies, stir, remove and cool. When cool, add sage (after crushing the leaves between the palms), pepper and salt, and mix well. Divide into 12 equal portions.

THE STUFFING: Flatten each ball between the palms, place a portion of the filling in the middle and make balls again.

THE KOFTA: Heat oil in a *kadhai*/wok and deep fry over medium heat until light golden. Remove to absorbent paper to drain the excess fat. (Fry only when the gravy is ready.)

THE GARNISH: Heat cream in pan, add almonds, stir over medium heat for 30 seconds.

COOKING

Heat butter in a *handi*/pan, add the garlic and ginger pastes (dissolved in 100ml/7 Tbs of water), *bhunno*/stir-fry until the moisture has evaporated, add tomato purée, red chillies and cashew nut paste, and *bhunno*/stir-fry for 4-5 minutes. Then add green cardamom, black cardamom, clove, cinnamon, mace, salt and fenugreek (after crushing the leaves between the palms), stir. Reduce to low heat, stir-in cream, remove and adjust the seasoning.

TO SERVE

Arrange the kofta in the middle of each of 4 individual plates, pour on equal quantities of gravy, garnish with equal quantities of the almond-cream mixture and serve with Naan or a bread of your choice.

———————— • ————————

ALOOBUKHARA KOFTA

INGREDIENTS

The Kofta

500g/1lb 2oz *Lauki*/Bottle Gourd
 (peel & grate)
Salt
100g/3 oz *Besan*/Gramflour
2 Green Chillies (seed & finely chop)
10g/1" piece Ginger (finely chop)

1.5g/½ tsp Black Pepper
 (freshly roasted & coarsely ground)
16 *Aloobukhara*/Dried Plums
16 Almonds (blanch, cool & peel)
Groundnut oil to deep fry kofta

The Gravy

50g/¼ cup *Desi Ghee*/Clarified Butter
3 *Chotti Elaichi*/Green Cardamom
2 *Lavang*/Cloves

3g/1 tsp Red Chilli Powder
1.5g/½ tsp *Haldee*/Turmeric Powder
720ml/3 cups Fresh Tomato Purée

1 stick *Daalcheeni*/Cinnamon (1")
1 *Tej Patta*/Bay Leaf
100g/3 oz Onions (grate)
20g/3¼tsp Garlic Paste (strain)
15g/2½ tsp Ginger Paste (strain)
9g/1 Tbs *Dhania*/Coriander Powder

Salt
1.5g/½ tsp *Motti Elaichi*/
  Black Cardamom Powder
A generous pinch of *Kasoori Methi*/
  Dried Fenugreek Leaf Powder
3.25g/1 Tbs *Taaza Dhania*/Coriander

Serves: 4
Preparation Time: 50-55 minutes
Cooking Time: 20-25 minutes

PREPARATION

THE GOURD: Put in a *handi*/pan, add a little salt and boil until cooked. Drain and then squeeze in a napkin to ensure it is completely devoid of moisture.

THE PLUMS: Remove pits and replace them with almonds.

THE KOFTA: Mix gramflour, green chillies, ginger, pepper and salt with gourd, knead well, divide into 16 equal portions and make balls. Flatten the balls between the palms, place a stuffed plum in the middle and make balls again. Heat oil in a *kadhai*/wok and deep fry kofta over medium heat until golden brown. Drain and remove to absorbent paper to drain excess fat.

COOKING

Heat ghee in a *handi*/pan, add cardamom, cloves, cinnamon and bay leaf, stir over medium heat until cardamom begins to change colour, add onions and sauté until translucent and glossy. Add ginger and garlic pastes, and sauté until onions become light pink. Then add coriander, red chilli and turmeric powders (dissolved in 45ml/3 Tbs of water), and *bhunno*/stir-fry until the moisture evaporates. Now add tomato purée, *bhunno*/stir-fry until specks of fat begin to appear on the surface, add water (approx 240ml/1 cup), bring to a boil, reduce to low heat and simmer, stirring occasionally, for 2-3 minutes. Add fried kofta, and simmer for 2 minutes. Sprinkle cardamom and kasoori methi powders, stir, remove and adjust the seasoning. Sprinkle coriander.

KHUMB te MUTTAR di SUBZI

INGREDIENTS

400g/14 oz Button Mushrooms (small)

400g/14 oz Green Peas (boil until cooked, but not soft-should be crisp)

50g/¼ cup *Desi Ghee*/Clarified Butter

2g/1 tsp *Jeera*/Cumin Seeds

8 flakes Garlic (finely chop)

200g/7 oz Onions (chop)

15g/1½" piece Ginger (finely chop)

4 Green Chillies (seed & halve lengthways)

15g/5 tsp *Amchoor*/Mango Powder

6g/2 tsp *Dhania*/Coriander Powder

3g/1 tsp Black Pepper (freshly roasted & coarsely ground)

1.5g/½ tsp *Chotti Elaichi*/ Green Cardamom Powder

0.75g/¼ tsp *Motti Elaichi*/ Black Cardamom Powder

0.75g/¼ tsp *Daalcheeni*/Cinnamon Powder

0.75g/¼ tsp *Lavang*/Clove Powder

A generous pinch of *Kasoori Methi*/ Dried Fenugreek Leaf Powder

Salt

3.25g/1 Tbs *Taaza Dhania*/Coriander (finely chop)

15ml/1 Tbs Lemon Juice

60g/2 oz Tomatoes (dice)

30g/1 oz *Paneer* (grate)

Serves: 4
Preparation Time: 25 minutes
Cooking Time: 45 minutes

COOKING

Heat ghee in a *kadhai*/wok, add cumin, stir over medium heat until it begins to pop, add garlic, sauté until it begins to change colour, add onions and sauté until light golden. Add ginger and green chillies, stir for a few seconds, add amchoor and coriander—dissolved in 45ml/3 Tbs of water—and *bhunno*/stir-fry until the moisture evaporates. Then add mushrooms, *bhunno*/stir-fry until the fat leaves the sides, add peas, stir, add pepper, green cardamom, black cardamom, cloves, kasoori methi and salt, *bhunno*/stir-fry until the masala coats mushrooms and peas. Now add chopped coriander and lemon juice, stir to mix well, remove and adjust the seasoning.

TO SERVE

Remove to service dish, garnish with tomato dices and paneer, and serve with Phulka or Poori.

SUBZ PUNJRATTANEE

INGREDIENTS

16 Baby Corn
4 Artichoke Hearts (quarter, wash
   and pat dry)
2 Palm Hearts (wash and cut into roundels)
32 Mushrooms
1 *Laal Shimla Mirch*/Red Bell Peppers
   (¼" thick strips)
1 *Peeli Shimla Mirch*/Yellow Bell Peppers
   (large; ¼" strips)
45ml/3 Tbs *Sarson*/Mustard Oil
100g/3 oz Onions (finely chop)

8 flakes Garlic (finely chop)
6.5g/2 Tbs *Taaza Dhania*/Coriander
   (finely chop)
3g/1½ tsp *Dhania*/Coriander Seeds
   (broiled & pounded)
3g/1 tsp Black Pepper Powder
   (freshly & coarsely ground)
Salt
120ml/½ cup Tomato Purée
10g/1" piece Ginger (juliennes)

Serves: 4
Preparation Time: 20 minutes
Cooking Time: 10-12 minutes

PREPARATION

THE MUSHROOMS: Remove the earthy base of the stalks, wash to remove grit and pat dry. (Here's a pro's tip: blanch mushrooms, which will make them tastier).

The recipe: Put 1 litre/4¼ cups of water in a *handi*/pan, add 120ml/½ cup of vinegar, 8 cloves, 2 sticks of cinnamon of 1", 2 bay leaves and 2 Tbs of salt and bring to a boil. Then add the mushrooms, bring to a boil again, reduce to low heat and simmer for 10 minutes. Drain and leave in a sieve to allow the liquor to drain out completely. This method leaves the mushrooms firm and, when completely devoid of moisture, they can be stored in glass jars for a few days.

COOKING

Heat mustard oil to a smoking point, remove, cool, reheat, add onions, sauté over medium heat until translucent and glossy, add garlic and sauté until onions are light golden. Then add baby corn, artichokes, palm hearts, mushrooms and bell peppers, increase to high heat and *bhunno*/ stir-fry for 4-5 minutes or until the baby corn, artichokes and palm hearts are al dente, add tomato purée and *bhunno*/stir-fry for 1-1½ minutes or until the purée nappes vegetables. Now sprinkle, coriander seeds, pepper and salt, stir, add tomatoes and coriander, stir for 1-1½ minutes. Remove and adjust the seasoning.

TO SERVE

Remove to service dish, garnish with ginger juliennes and serve either as an entré with Phulka, Chappati or Tandoori Roti or as an accompaniment.

———————— • ————————

BESAN naal BHUNE BHEIN te ALOO

INGREDIENTS

800g/1lb 13 oz *Bhein/Nadru*/Lotus
   Root Stems
250g/9 oz Potatoes (cut into ¼" thick
   slices; boil until al dente)
120g/10 Tbs *Desi Ghee*/Clarified Butter
150g/5 oz *Besan*/Gramflour
3g/1 tsp *Amchoor*/Mango Powder
3g/1 tsp Red Chilli Powder
Salt
1.5g/½ tsp Black Pepper
   (freshly roasted & coarsely ground)

0.75g/¼ tsp *Motti Elaichi*/
   Black Cardamom Powder
0.75g/¼ tsp *Daalcheeni*/Cinnamon Powder
0.75g/¼ tsp *Lavang*/Clove Powder
0.75g/¼ tsp *Jaiphal*/Nutmeg Powder
15ml/1 Tbs Lemon Juice
2 Green Chillies (seed & cut into juliennes)
3.25g/1 Tbs *Taaza Dhania*/Coriander (chop)

Serves: 4
Preparation Time: 45 minutes
Cooking Time: 5 minutes

PREPARATION

THE LOTUS ROOTS: Peel, rinse thoroughly to remove grit—there'll be plenty of it—and cut into ¼" thick slices cut at a 45° slant. Then put in a *handi*/pan, add salt and enough water, and boil until tender. Drain and cool.

Subz Punjrattanee (*Stir-fry*)

Bharwaan Karele (*Veg. Entre*)

Baingan ka Bhartha (*Veg. Entre*)

Sukki Bhindee (*Stir-fry*)

Aloo Vadhi (*Popular traditional fare*)

Chhole Aloo (*Stir-fry*)

Pakorhe Aloo te Pyaazwali Kadhi (*Popular traditional fare*)

Kadhai de Jheengey te Asparagus (*Stir-fry*)

COOKING

Heat ghee in a *kadhai*/wok; add gramflour and *bhunno*/stir-fry until it emits its unique aroma. Then add bhein, potatoes and the remaining ingredients, except lemon juice and coriander, *bhunno*/stir-fry delicately with a spatula until the gramflour coats the bhein and potatoes. Sprinkle lemon juice, stir carefully, remove and adjust the seasoning.

TO SERVE

Remove to a flat dish, garnish with green chillies and coriander and serve as an accompaniment.

•

BHARWAAN KARELE BHOR NAAL

INGREDIENTS

12 *Karela*/Bitter Gourd
Salt
75ml/5 Tbs *Sarson*/Mustard Oil
6 flakes Garlic
20g/2" piece Ginger
12 Pearl Onions

2.25g/¾ tsp *Anaardaana*/
   Dried Pomegranate Powder
A generous pinch of Black Pepper
   (freshly roasted & coarsely ground)
5ml/1tsp Lemon Juice

The Filling

150g/5 oz Potatoes (dice & parboil)
4.5g/1½ tsp *Anaardaana*/
   Dried Pomegranate Powder
2.25g/¾ tsp Black Pepper
   (freshly roasted & coarsely ground)
15ml/1 Tbs *Sarson*/Mustard Oil

45g/1½ oz *Paneer* (grate)
30g/1 oz Cheese (grate)
2 Green Chillies (seed & chop)
3.25g/1 Tbs *Taaza Dhania*/Coriander (chop)
Salt

Serves: 4
Preparation Time: 2:15 hours
Cooking Time: 1:45 hours

PREPARATION

THE BITTER GOURD: Wash, scrape and reserve the scrapings/rough skin-*bhor*. Then slit on one side to create pockets, remove the seeds, rub both the bitter gourd and the bhor with salt, arrange on a tilting tray and reserve for at least an hour. (This is done to reduce the bitterness. If you don't think you can handle even this little bitterness, reserve the bitter gourd overnight). Now wash both in running water to remove the salt. Drain. Put bhor in a napkin and squeeze out the excess moisture.

THE FILLING: Heat oil to smoking point in a *kadhai*/wok, remove and cool. Re-heat oil, add pomegranate and pepper, and stir over medium heat for a few seconds. Then add potato dices, and sauté until light golden. Remove, cool, add the remaining ingredients, mix well, and divide into 12 equal portions.

THE STUFFING: Pack a portion of the filling in each bitter gourd, secure with string (to prevent the filling from spilling out) and keep aside.

COOKING

Heat oil to smoking point in a *kadhai*/wok, remove and cool. Re-heat oil, add garlic, stir over medium heat for a few seconds, add ginger and sauté until the garlic is golden brown. Reduce to low heat, add the stuffed bitter gourd, cover and cook, turning over at regular intervals, for 30 minutes. Then add bhor, onions, pomegranate and salt, cover and cook, stirring and turning at regular intervals, for an hour. Remove, sprinkle pepper and adjust the seasoning.

TO SERVE

Remove to a serving dish and serve with Tandoori Roti and Moong ki Daal.

———————— • ————————

BHARTHA

INGREDIENTS

4 *Baingan* / Brinjals (large *Bhurtha Baingan*)
Groundnut oil to brush *Baingan*/Brinjals
8 flakes Garlic
8 *Lavang*/Cloves
100g/½ cup *Desi Ghee*/Clarified Butter
2g/1 tsp *Jeera*/Cumin Seeds
250g/9 oz Onions (chop)

10g/1" piece Ginger (chop)
4 Green Chillies (seed & chop)
3g/1 tsp Red Chilli Powder
1.5g/½ tsp *Haldee*/Turmeric Powder
350g/13 oz Tomatoes (chop)
Salt
6.5g/2 Tbs *Taaza Dhania*/Coriander (chop)

Serves: 4
Preparation Time: 45 minutes
Cooking Time: 25 minutes

PREPARATION

THE BRINJALS: Stud each brinjal with 2 flakes of garlic and 2 cloves, and brush with ghee. There are three ways to roast: place the brinjal on embers of charcoal, on an angeethi or tandoor, and turning at regular intervals, until the skin becomes black, skewering and roasting, as above, in a tandoor on low heat or over low heat on a gas range, also as above.

Remove, discard the cloves, transfer to a panful of water, cool, peel the blackened skin and mash the flesh.

COOKING

Heat ghee in a *kadhai*/wok, add cumin, stir over medium heat until it begins to pop, add onions, and sauté until transparent. Then add ginger and green chillies, sauté for a few seconds, add brinjals, red chillies and turmeric, and *bhunno*/stir-fry until fat leaves the sides. Now add tomatoes and salt, *bhunno*/stir-fry until fat leaves the sides. Remove and adjust the seasoning.

TO SERVE

Remove to a serving dish, garnish with coriander and serve with Tandoori Paratha.

SUKKI BHINDEE

INGREDIENTS

600g/1 lb 5 oz *Bhindee*/Okra (small)
16 Pearl Onions (peel)

50g/¼ cup *Desi Ghee*/Clarified Butter

The Filling

25g/2 Tbs *Desi Ghee*/Clarified Butter
9g/1 Tbs *Amchoor*/Mango Powder
4.5g/1½ tsp *Dhania*/Coriander Powder
4.5g/1½ tsp *Saunf*/Fennel Powder
3g/1 tsp *Jeera*/Cumin Powder
3g/1 tsp Black Pepper
 (freshly roasted & coarsely ground)

3g/1 tsp Red Chilli Powder
3g/1 tsp *Haldee*/Turmeric Powder
1.5g/½ tsp *Motti Elaichi*/
 Black Cardamom Powder
3g/1tsp *Kala Namak*/Black Salt
0.75g/¼ tsp *Jaiphal*/Nutmeg Powder
Salt

The Garnish

Red Chillies (seeded & cut into juliennes)

Ginger juliennes reserved in lemon juice

Serves: 4
Preparation Time: 30 minutes
Cooking Time: 15-20 minutes

PREPARATION

THE OKRA: Slice off the caps and the tips, slit, seed and keep aside.

THE FILLING: Mix all the ingredients in a bowl.

THE STUFFING: Pack the okra with equal quantities of the filling.

COOKING

Heat ghee in a *kadhai*/wok, add the stuffed okra, cover and cook over medium heat, stirring occasionally, for 5-6 minutes. Reduce to very low heat, add onions, cover and cook, stirring occasionally, for 9-10 minutes or until okra and onions are cooked, but firm. Remove and adjust the seasoning.

TO SERVE

Remove to a flat dish, garnish with red chilli and ginger juliennes, and serve with Paratha or Phulka.

—————————— • ——————————

DAHIWALI BHINDEE

INGREDIENTS

600g/1 lb 5 oz *Bhindee*/Okra (small)
25g/2 Tbs *Desi Ghee*/Clarified Butter
9g/1 Tbs *Amchoor*/Mango Powder
4.5g/1½ tsp *Dhania*/Coriander Powder
4.5g/1½ tsp *Saunf*/Fennel Powder
3g/1 tsp *Jeera*/Cumin Powder
3g/1 tsp Black Pepper (freshly roasted & coarsely ground)

3g/1 tsp Red Chilli Powder
3g/1 tsp *Haldee*/Turmeric Powder
1.5g/½ tsp *Motti Elaichi*/Black Cardamom Powder
0.75g/¼ tsp *Jaiphal*/Nutmeg Powder
Salt

The Gravy

50g/¼ cup *Desi Ghee*/Clarified Butter
150g/5 oz Onions (slice)
3g/1 tsp Red Chilli Powder

1.5g/½ tsp *Haldee*/Turmeric Powder
720ml/3 cups Yoghurt (whisk)
Salt

The Garnish

Red Chillies (seeded & cut into juliennes)   Ginger juliennes reserved in lemon juice

Serves: 4
Preparation Time: 30 minutes
Cooking Time: 15-20 minutes

PREPARATION

THE OKRA: Slice off the caps and the tips, slit, seed and keep aside.

THE FILLING: Mix all the ingredients in a bowl.

THE STUFFING: Pack the okra with equal quantities of the filling.

COOKING

Heat *ghee* in a *kadhai*/wok, add onions and sauté over low heat until translucent and glossy (ensure that the onions *do not* get coloured). Then add red chillies and turmeric (dissolved in 30ml/2 Tbs of water), *bhunno*/stir-fry until the moisture evaporates, add the stuffed okra, cover and cook over medium heat, stirring occasionally, for 7-8 minutes. Remove *handi*/pan from heat, stir-in yoghurt and salt, return *handi*/pan to heat and cook, stirring occasionally, but carefully (to ensure that the filling does not ooze out completely), until of custard consistency. Remove and adjust the seasoning.

TO SERVE

Remove to a flat dish, garnish with red chilli and ginger juliennes, and serve with Paratha or Phulka.

———————————— • ————————————

ADRAK te GOBHI da KHEEMA

INGREDIENTS

1Kg/2 lb 2oz Cauliflower
    (cut into very small florets)
Cooking Oil to fry
20g/2" piece Ginger (finely chopped)
5 Green Chilli (deseeded and chopped fine)

1.5g/½ tsp *Motti Elaichi*/
    Black Cardamom Powder
0.75g/¼ tsp *Lavang*/Clove Powder
A generous pinch of *Kasoori Methi*/
    Dried Fenugreek Leaf Powder

3g/1tsp *Jeera*/Cumin Seeds
3g/1 tsp *Haldee* / Turmeric Powder
6g/2tsp Red Chilli Powder
75g/³⁄₈ cup *Desi Ghee*/ Clarified Butter
120g/ ½ cup *Dahi*/ Yoghurt
6.5g/2Tbsp *Taaza Dhania*/
   Coriander Leaves (chopped fine)

3g/1tsp *Daalcheeni*/ Cinnamon Powder
5g/1½ tsp *Jeera*/Cumin Powder
1.5g/½ tsp Black Pepper
   (freshly roasted & coarsely ground)
10g/ 1" piece Ginger Juliennes
15ml/1Tbs Lemon Juice
Salt

Serves: 4
Preparation Time: 25 minutes
Cooking Time: 7-8 minutes

COOKING

Marinate the cauliflower florets with salt and half of the turmeric powder. Heat oil in a *kadhai*/ wok. Deep fry cauliflower florets over medium heat, until golden brown. Drain and remove to absorbent paper to drain excess fat.

Heat ghee in a *handi*/pan, add cumin seeds and stir till it starts to crackle. Add the fine chopped green chillies, the fine chopped ginger and the fried cauliflower florets. Stir for a minute and then add the rest of the turmeric, red chilli and the jeera powder. Now, add the whisked yoghurt and cook on a medium fire until the moisture evaporates and the gravy nappes the florets. Sprinkle cinnamon, black pepper, kasuri methi, clove, and cardamom powders and stir. Finish with lemon, juice stir and remove.

TO SERVE

Garnish with ginger juliennes, chopped fresh coriander and serve hot with Roti.

———————— • ————————

MASALEDAAR ARBI

INGREDIENTS

20 *Arbi*/Colocassia
   (medium; approx 1 Kg/2¼ lb)
30ml/2 Tbs Lemon Juice
Mustard Oil to deep fry Colocassia
75ml/5 Tbs Mustard Oil

6g/2 tsp Red Chilli Powder
1.5g/½ tsp *Haldee*/Turmeric Powder
30g/1 oz Cashew nut Paste
1.5g/½ tsp *Chotti Elaichi*/
   Green Cardamom Powder

2g/1 tsp *Jeera*/Cumin Seeds
1.5g/1tsp *Methidaana*/Fenugreek Seeds
3g/2tsp *Saunf*/Fennel Powder
250g/9 oz Onions
20g/3¼ tsp Ginger Paste (strain)
10g/1¾ tsp Garlic Paste (strain)
450ml/2 cups *Dhania*/Coriander Powder

1.5 g/½ tsp *Shahi Jeera*/
  Black Cumin Powder
0.375g/⅛ tsp *Daalcheeni*/
  Cinnamon Powder
0.375g/⅛ tsp *Lavang*/Clove Powder
Salt
10ml/2 tsp Lemon Juice

The Garnish

2 Green Chillies
3.25g/1 Tbs *Dhania*/Coriander

Ginger Juliennes reserved in lemon juice

Serves: 4
Preparation Time: 1 hour
Cooking Time: 35 minutes

PREPARATION

THE COLOCASSIA: Wash thoroughly, put in a *handi*/pan, cover with enough water, boil until cooked, add lemon juice, bring to a boil again, drain, cool, peel and reserve in a panful of water. Heat mustard oil to a smoking point in a *lagan*/flat pan (or *kadhai*/wok), remove, cool, reheat, add the boiled colocassia and deep fry over medium heat until golden and crisp. Remove to absorbent paper to drain excess fat. (Reserve 75ml/5 Tbs of oil for the gravy.)

THE ONIONS: Peel, wash and finely chop.

THE YOGHURT MIXTURE: Whisk in a bowl, add coriander, red chilli and turmeric powders, whisk to homogenise.

THE GARNISH: Wash green chillies, slit, seed, cut into juliennes and discard the stems. Clean, wash, and finely chop coriander.

COOKING

Heat mustard oil to a smoking point in a *lagan*/flat pan (or *kadhai*/wok), remove, cool, reheat, add cumin and methi seeds, stir over medium heat until they begin to pop. Add onions, sauté until translucent and glossy, add ginger and garlic pastes, *bhunno*/stir-fry until the onions are golden (not golden brown), add the yoghurt mixture, *bhunno*/stir-fry until the fat leaves the sides, add the cashew nut paste and *bhunno*/stir-fry until the fat leaves the sides. Then add 480ml/2 cups of water, bring to a boil, reduce to low heat, sprinkle green cardamom, black cumin, cinnamon, clove, fennel powders, stir, add salt, stir, cover with a lid and cook on *dum* for 20 minutes (the gravy should nappe the colocassia). Remove, sprinkle lemon juice, stir, and adjust the seasoning.

TO SERVE

Remove to a flat dish, garnish with green chillies, coriander and ginger juliennes, serve with Paratha.

————————— • —————————

ALOO VADIYAN

INGREDIENTS

4 Potatoes (cut into old-fashioned
    finger chips)
250g/9 oz *Vadi* (*Urad Daal*; deep fry in
    oil and reserve in water)
65g/5 Tbs *Desi Ghee*/Clarified Butter
4g/2 tsp *Jeera*/Cumin Seeds
150g/5 oz Onions (chop)
20g/3½ tsp Ginger Paste (strain)
10g/1¾ tsp Garlic Paste (strain)

150ml/5 oz Yoghurt
9g/1 Tbs *Dhania*/Coriander Powder
3g/1 tsp Red Chilli Powder
3g/1 tsp *Haldee*/Turmeric Powder
150ml/5 oz Fresh Tomato Purée
Salt
A generous pinch *Kasoori Methi*/
    Fenugreek Powder
3.25g/1 Tbs *Taaza Dhania*/Coriander (chop)

Serves: 4
Preparation Time: 45 minutes
Cooking Time: 30 minutes

PREPARATION

THE YOGHURT MIXTURE: Put yoghurt in a bowl, add coriander, red chilli and turmeric, whisk to mix well.

COOKING

Heat ghee in a *kadhai*/wok, add cumin seeds, and stir over medium heat until they begin to pop. Add onions, sauté until light golden, and add garlic and ginger pastes, *bhunno*/stir fry until onions are golden. Remove *handi*/pan from heat, stir-in the yoghurt mixture, return *handi*/pan to heat and *bhunno*/stir-fry until specks of fat begin to appear on the surface. Then add tomato purée and potatoes, and *bhunno*/stir-fry until fat leaves the sides. Add 1 litre/4¼ cups of water and salt and bring to a boil; reduce to low heat and simmer, stirring occasionally, until potatoes are three-fourths cooked. Now drain and add vadi, bring to a boil, reduce to low heat and simmer, stirring occasionally, until the potatoes are cooked and the gravy is of a thin sauce consistency. Sprinkle kasoori methi, stir, remove and adjust the seasoning.

TO SERVE

Remove to a service dish, garnish with coriander and serve with Phulka.

— • —

CHHOLE ALOO

INGREDIENTS

250g/1¼ cups White Gram
450g/1 lb Potatoes
Oil to fry
110g/½ cup *Desi Ghee*/Clarified Butter
3g/1tsp *Jeera*/Cumin Seeds
30g/5tsp Garlic Paste

A pinch of Soda bi-carb
Salt
750g/3½ cups Tomatoes
30ml/2 Tbs Lemon Juice
5g/1tsp *Amchoor* Powder/
    dried mango powder

The Bouquet Garni

4 *Motti Elaichi*/Black Cardamom
2 sticks *Dalcheeni*/Cinnamon
2 *Tej Patta*/Bay Leaves
10g/5tsp *Taaza Dhania*/Coriander Seeds
    (freshly broiled and crushed)

4 Green Chillies
40g/ ¼ cup Ginger
30g/ ½ cup Coriander
6.5g/ 2tsp *Deghi Mirch* Powder

The Garnish

10g/1Tbsp Ginger
4 Green Chillies
5g/1 tsp *Amchoor* Powder
10g/2tsp *Garam Masala*

Salt
Ghee to shallow fry
3g/ ¾ tsp *Kasoori Methi*/Fenugreek

Serves: 4
Preparation Time: 55 minutes
Cooking Time: 20-24 minutes

PREPARATION

THE WHITE GRAM: Pick, wash, soak overnight in a *handi*, drain and replenish with fresh water. Add soda bi-carb and salt and bring to a boil, reduce to low heat, immerse the bouquet garni, cover and simmer until gram is tender. Drain.

THE VEGETABLES: Pel, wash and cut into 1½" dices. Heat oil in a *kadhai* and deep fry over medium heat until three-fourths cooked and light brown in colour. Remove.

Wash and chop tomatoes. Remove stems, wash, slit, deseed and chop the green chillies. Scrape, wash and chop ginger. Clean, wash and chop coriander.

THE GARNISH: Scrape, wash and cut ginger into fine juliennes. Wash green chillies, make a slit on one side. Mix mango powder and salt and stuff the slit chillies with this mixture.

Heat ghee in a frying pan and shallow fry the ginger juliennes over medium heat until golden brown. Remove. In the same oil shallow fry the green chillies until they become bright green (approx one minute)

COOKING

Heat ghee in a *kadhai*/wok, add cumin seeds and sauté, add onions and sauté until light brown. Add the chopped ginger and the chopped green chillies and *bhunno*/stir-fry for a couple of minutes. Add the garlic paste and sauté. Add deghi mirch powder and sauté till the fat leaves the sides. Add the boiled white gram and reduce to medium heat. Add tomatoes and simmer stirring occasionally until fat leaves the masala. Add the fried potato dices and *bhunno*/stir-fry for another five minutes. Adjust the seasoning. Sprinkle garam masala, amchoor powder, lemon juice, fenugreek, and stir.

TO SERVE

Serve hot in a bowl garnished with the ginger juliennes, stuffed green chillies and chopped coriander.

PAKORHE ALOO te PYAAZWALI KADHI

INGREDIENTS

The Kadhi

900g/3½ cups Yoghurt (1-day old)
90g/3 oz Besan/Gramflour
3g/1 tsp Red Chilli Powder
1.5g/½ tsp Haldee/Turmeric Powder
Salt

50g/¼ cup Desi Ghee/Clarified Butter
1g/¼ tsp Methidaana/Fenugreek Seeds
200g/7 oz Potatoes (thin roundels)
150g/5 oz Onions (thin roundels)

The Pakorha

100g/3 oz Besan/Gramflour
300/11 oz Spinach (shred)
A pinch of Soda Bi-carb
Salt
2g/1 tsp Dhania/Coriander Seeds
   (pound gently to split)

1.25g/½ tsp Ajwain/Carom
10g/1" piece Ginger (finely chop)
4 Green Chillies (finely chop)
Cooking Oil to deep fry Pakorha

The Tempering

75g/6 Tbs Mustard Oil
2g/1 tsp Jeera/Cumin Seeds
1g/½ tsp Dhania/Coriander Seeds

A generous pinch of Heeng/Asafoetida
4 Whole Dried Red Chillies
1.5g/½ tsp Red Chilli Powder

Serves: 4
Preparation Time: 2:20 hours
Cooking Time: 2:15 hours

PREPARATION

THE KADHI: Whisk yoghurt in a bowl; add besan, red chillies, turmeric and salt, and whisk to mix well. Then add 1.2 litres/5 cups of water and whisk again. (To get a Kadhi of better consistency, forget about yoghurt. Instead, use 1.7 litres/7 cups of chchaas/butter milk.)

THE PAKORHA: Mix all the ingredients, add water (approx 45ml/3 Tbs) and mix well. Heat oil in a kadhai/wok, mentally divide the batter into 20 equal portions, and make dumplings and deep fry over medium heat until golden. Remove to absorbent paper to drain the excess fat.

COOKING

Heat desi ghee in a *handi*/pan, add fenugreek seeds and stir over medium heat until they begin to pop. Add yoghurt (or buttermilk) mixture and bring to a boil, stirring continuously. Reduce to low heat, cover and simmer, stirring occasionally, until of thin sauce consistency. Then add potato roundels, bring to a boil, reduce to low heat and simmer, stirring occasionally, until potatoes are cooked (approx 5-6 minutes). Now add pakorha and onion roundels, bring to a boil, and reduce to low heat and simmer, stirring occasionally, but carefully, until the Kadhi attains a thick sauce consistency. Remove and adjust the seasoning.

To prepare the tempering, heat mustard oil in a frying pan, add the cumin and coriander seeds, stir over medium heat until they begin to pop. Then add asafoetida and stir until it puffs up, add whole red chillies and stir until they change colour (bright red). Now add chilli powder, stir, remove and pour over the Kadhi.

TO SERVE

Remove to a bowl and serve with Steamed Rice.

KADHAI de JHEENGEY te TAAZE ASPARAGUS

INGREDIENTS

20 Prawns (medium)
16 spears Asparagus
75ml/5 Tbs Chilli Oil
24 *Kaari Patta*/Curry Leaf
4 Whole Red Chillies
    (dried; seed & cut into strips)

4.5g/1½ tsp *Dhania*/Coriander Powder
3g/1 tsp Red Chilli Powder
1.5g/½ tsp *Haldee*/Turmeric Powder
Salt
30g/1 oz Sweet Mango Chutney (juliennes)
2 Leeks (juliennes)

The Paste

1 Onion (large)
30g/ 1 oz *Narial*/Coconut
    (remove brown skin & grate)
8 flakes Garlic (roughly chop)
10g/1" piece Ginger (roughly chop)

15g/½ oz *Imlee*/Tamarind Pulp
    (reserve in 45ml/3 Tbs of hot water)
9g/1 Tbs *Khus-khus*/Poppy Seeds
    (reserve in hot water)

Serves: 4
Preparation Time: 1 hour
Cooking Time: 9-10 minutes

PREPARATION

THE PRAWNS: Shell but retain the tails, vein, wash and pat dry.

THE ASPARAGUS: String and cut tips along with ½" of the stem; slice the remaining stems diagonally, discarding the tough ends.

THE PASTE: Roast onions on charcoal until the skin is black (approx 4-5 minutes), remove, cool, peel and roughly chop. Transfer to a blender, add tamarind along with the water, poppy seeds after draining the water and the remaining ingredients, and pulse to make a smooth paste.

COOKING

Heat oil in a *kadhai*/wok, add curry leaf, stir until it stops spluttering, add whole red chillies and stir until they begin to change colour. Add coriander, red chilli and turmeric powders (dissolved in 45ml/3 Tbs of water), *bhunno*/stir-fry until the moisture evaporates, add the paste and salt, and *bhunno*/stir-fry until the fat leaves the sides. Then add prawns and asparagus, *bhunno*/stir-fry for a minute, add mango and leek juliennes, and *bhunno*/stir-fry for another minute. Remove and adjust the seasoning.

TAMATERWALE JHEENGEY

INGREDIENTS

24 Prawns (24-26 Kg; shell & vein)
62.5g/5 Tbs *Desi Ghee*/Clarified Butter
3 *Motti Elaichi*/Black Cardamom
2 stick *Daalcheeni*/Cinnamon (1")
2 *Tej Patta*/Bay Leaf
12 flakes Garlic (chop)
10g/1" piece Ginger (chop)
4.5g/1½ tsp Kashmiri Deghi Mirch Powder

1 litre/4¼ cups Fresh Tomato Purée
Salt
1.5g/½ tsp *Motti Elaichi*/
   Black Cardamom Powder
0.75g/¼ tsp *Daalcheeni*/Cinnamon Powder
A generous pinch of *Kasoori Methi*/
   Dried Fenugreek Leaf Powder

The Garnish

16 Tomato Slices (from medium tomatoes)
60ml/¼ cup Cream

2 Green Chillies (chop)
3.25g/1 Tbs *Taaza Dhania*/Coriander (chop)

Serves: 4
Preparation Time: 45 minutes
Cooking Time: 25 minutes

COOKING

Heat 50g/¼ cup of ghee in a *handi*/pan, add cardamom, cinnamon and bay leaf, stir over medium heat for a minute, add garlic, sauté until it begins to change colour (it should not become light golden), add ginger and sauté until garlic is light golden. Then add deghi mirch, stir, add tomato purée and salt, *bhunno*/stir-fry until specks of fat begin to appear on the surface, add water (480ml/2 cups), bring to a boil, reduce to low heat and simmer, stirring occasionally, until reduced by a quarter.

To cook the prawns, heat the remaining ghee in a separate *handi*/pan, add prawns and sauté over high heat for a minute. Add the simmering gravy, sprinkle cardamom, cinnamon and kasoori methi, stir, remove and adjust the seasoning.

To prepare the garnish, heat cream over high heat in a frying pan, add the remaining ingredients and stir for a minute.

TO SERVE

Remove to service bowl, garnish with tomato slices, pour on the remaining cream mixture and serve with Steamed Rice or Roti.

PATIALASHAHI MACHCHI

INGREDIENTS

1 Kg/2¼ lb Singhara or Sole (2" boned cubes)

The Marination

30g/5 tsp Garlic Paste (strain)
20g/3½ tsp Ginger Paste (strain)
30ml/2 Tbs Lemon Juice

1.5g/½ tsp Red Chilli Powder
Salt

The Gravy

75g/6 Tbs *Desi Ghee*/Clarified Butter
200g/3 oz Onions (finely chop)
8 flakes Garlic (finely chop)
10g/1" piece Ginger (finely chop)
4 Green Chillies (seed & finely chop)
3g/1 tsp Red Chilli Powder
1.5g/½ tsp *Haldee*/Turmeric Powder
Salt
100g/3 oz Tomatoes (finely chop)
120g/½ cup Yoghurt (whisk)

2 *Tej Patta*/Bay Leaf
0.75g/¼ tsp *Motti Elaichi*/
   Black Cardamom Powder
0.75g/¼ tsp Black Pepper
   (freshly roasted & coarsely ground)
0.375g/⅛ tsp *Daalcheeni*/
   Cinnamon Powder
0.375g/⅛ tsp *Lavang*/Clove Powder
15ml/1 Tbs Lemon Juice
6.5g/2 Tbs *Taaza Dhania*/Coriander

Serves: 4
Preparation Time: 45 minutes
Cooking Time: 25 minutes

PREPARATION

THE MARINATION: Mix all the ingredients, evenly rub the fish cubes with this marinade and reserve for 30 minutes. (If you are not confident handling fish and feel that it might break up while cooking, then heat enough cooking oil in a *kadhai*/wok, add the marinated fish, deep fry over medium heat until lightly coloured, drain and remove to absorbent paper to drain excess fat.)

COOKING

Heat ghee in a *kadhai*/wok, add onions, sauté until light golden, add garlic and ginger, and sauté until onions are golden. Add red chilli and turmeric (dissolved in 30ml/2 Tbs of water), and *bhunno*/stir-fry until the moisture evaporates. Then add tomatoes and salt, *bhunno*/stir-fry until fat leaves the sides. Remove *kadhai*/wok from heat, stir-in yoghurt, return *kadhai*/wok to heat, *bhunno*/stir-fry until specks of fat begin to appear on the surface, add water (approx 720ml/3 cups), bring to a boil and then reduce to low heat. Wipe off the excess marinade, add fish and simmer until the fish is cooked and the gravy is of thin sauce consistency. Remove and adjust the seasoning.

TO SERVE

Remove to a service bowl and serve with Steamed Rice or Roti.

MACHCHI ANAARI

INGREDIENTS

8 fillets Sole (90g/3 oz each)

The Marination

30g/5 tsp Garlic Paste (strained)
20g/3½ tsp Ginger Paste (strained)
90ml/6 Tbs Pomegranate Juice

1.5g/½ tsp Red Chilli Powder
Salt

The Filling

150g/5 oz Prawns
150g/5 oz Sole Trimmings
60g/2 oz Pomegranate
5g/½" piece Ginger
3.25g/1 Tbs Coriander

2 Green Chillies
1g/½ tsp *Ajwain*/Carom
30ml/2 Tbs Cream
1 Egg White
Salt

The Gravy

45ml/3 Tbs Oil
3 *Lavang*/Cloves
2 *Tej Patta*/Bay Leaves
A generous pinch *Heeng*/Asafoetida
150g/5 oz Onions

1.5g/½ tsp Red Chilli Powder
120g/½ cup *Dahi*/Yoghurt
Salt
1.5g/½ tsp *Chhoti Elaichi*/Green
    Cardamom Powder

Tamaterwali Jheengey (*Non-Veg. Curry***)**

Mardaan Murg Malaaiwala (*Non-Veg. Curry***)**

Muttar Nukta (*Veg. Curry*)

Saagwala Meat (*Stir-fry*)

Nalliwala Meat (*Non-Veg. Curry*)

Magaz Masala (*Stir-fry*)

Meat Beliram (*Non-Veg. Curry*)

Thipparanwala Meat (*Non-Veg. Curry*)

30g/5 tsp Garlic Paste (strained)
15g/2½ tsp Ginger Paste (strained)
3g/1 tsp Turmeric Powder
1 litre/4¼ cups Fish Stock

1.5g/½ tsp Black Pepper Powder
1g/⅓ tsp Mace Powder
20ml/4 tsp Cream

Serves: 4
Preparation Time: 1:45 hours
Cooking Time: 25 minutes

PREPARATION

THE FISH FILLETS: Clean, trim, wash and pat dry.

THE MARINATION: Mix all the ingredients, evenly rub the fish fillets with this marinade and reserve for 10 minutes.

THE FILLING: Shell prawns, devein, wash and pat dry. Clean fish trimmings, wash and pat dry. Put these ingredients in a food processor/mincer and make a coarse mousse. Scrape, wash and finely chop ginger. Clean, wash and finely chop coriander. Remove stems, wash, slit, deseed and finely chop green chillies. Put these ingredients in a bowl, add the remaining ingredients, mix well and divide into 8 equal portions.

THE STUFFING: Spread a portion of the filling along the length on one side of each fillet, and roll to make paupiettes.

THE GRAVY: Dissolve asafoetida in 30ml/2 Tbs of lukewarm water. Peel, wash and finely chop onions. Whisk yoghurt in a bowl.

COOKING

Heat oil in a *handi*/pan, add cloves and bay leaves, stir over medium heat until the cloves begin to crackle, add asafoetida, stir, add onions, sauté until translucent and glossy, add the garlic and ginger pastes, *bhunno* /stir-fry for a minute, add turmeric, red chillies and salt (all dissolved in 30ml/2 Tbs of water), stir until the liquid has evaporated. Remove *handi*/pan from heat, stir-in yoghurt, return *handi*/pan to heat and *bhunno*/stir-fry until the fat leaves the sides. Now add fish stock, bring to a boil, reduce to low heat and simmer until reduced by a third. Remove and pass the gravy through fine muslin into a separate *handi*/pan. Return the gravy to heat, add salt, stir, gently add the paupiettes and simmer until the gravy is of sauce consistency. Sprinkle cardamom, black pepper and mace powders, stir carefully. Now stir-in cream, remove and adjust the seasoning.

TO SERVE

Arrange two fish paupiettes on each of four individual plates, pour on equal quantities of the gravy, arrange a garnish of your choice and serve with Tandoori Roti or Steamed Rice.

———————— • ————————

ATTOCKWALE BATAER MASALEDAAR

INGREDIENTS

8 *Bataer*/Quails (prick the surface with a fork)

75g/6 Tbs *Desi Ghee*/Clarified Butter

4 *Motti Elaichi*/Black Cardamom

4 *Lavang*/Cloves

2 sticks *Daalcheeni*/Cinnamon (1")

2 *Tej Patta*/Bay Leaf

8 flakes Garlic (finely chop)

250g/9 oz Onions (grate)

10g/1" piece Ginger (finely chop)

6g/2 tsp *Dhania*/Coriander Powder

3g/1 tsp Red Chilli Powder

120g/5 oz Tomato Purée

Salt

75ml/2½ oz Yoghurt (whisk)

30g/1 oz Almond Paste

1.5g/½ tsp *Chotti Elaichi*/ Green Cardamom Powder

0.75g/¼ tsp *Daalcheeni*/Cinnamon Powder

0.75g/¼ tsp *Lavang*/Clove Powder

0.75g/¼ tsp *Javitri*/Mace Powder

0.5g/½ tsp *Zaafraan*/Saffron

The Marination

90ml/6 Tbs Red Wine

30ml/2 Tbs *Sirka*/Malt Vinegar

20g/ 3¼ tsp Garlic Paste (strain)

15g/2½ tsp Ginger Paste (strain)

4.5g/1½ tsp Red Chilli Powder

Salt

The Filling

250g/9 oz Chicken Mince

8 flakes Garlic (finely chop)

7.5g/¾" Ginger (finely chop)

2 Green Chilli (finely chop)

16 Roasted Pistachio

16 *Kishmish*/Raisins (refresh in water until they puff up)

1.25g/½ tsp *Shahi Jeera*/Royal or Black Cumin Seeds

2.25g/¾ tsp Black Pepper (freshly roasted & coarsely ground)

1.5g/½ tsp *Chotti Elaichi*/ Green Cardamom Powder

0.75g/¼ tsp *Javitri*/Mace Powder

Salt

The Garnish

Flakes of Toasted Almonds
0.25g/¼ tsp *Zaafraan*/Saffron

Chandi ka Varq/Silver leaf

Serves: 4
Preparation Time: 2:15 hours
Cooking Time: 1 hour

PREPARATION

THE MARINATION: Mix all the ingredients, evenly rub the quails with this marinade and reserve for at least an hour.

THE FILLING: Mix all the ingredients and divide into 8 equal portions.

THE STUFFING: Stuff the abdominal cavity of the quails with a portion of the filling from the tail end, then double up the legs, ensuring that drumsticks cover the opening through which the filling was stuffed and tie firmly with string. Gently twist the winglet bones to make the birds more stable when they are placed on the plate at the time of service.

THE SAFFRON: Crush threads with a pestle or the back of a spoon, soak in water and then make a paste.

THE GARNISH: Reserve saffron flakes in lukewarm water and when the water turns saffron, reserve to almond flakes to enable them to acquire a saffron hue.

COOKING

Heat ghee in a *handi*/pan, add black cardamom, cloves, cinnamon and bay leaf, stir over medium heat for a few seconds, add garlic, sauté until it begins to change colour, add onions and sauté until onions are light golden. Add ginger, *bhunno*/stir-fry until onions are golden, add coriander and red chillies (dissolved in 30ml/2 Tbs of water), and *bhunno*/stir-fry until the moisture evaporates. Then add tomato purée and salt, and *bhunno*/stir-fry until the fat leaves the sides. Remove *handi*/pan from heat, stir-in yoghurt, return *handi*/pan to heat, *bhunno*/stir-fry over medium heat until specks of fat begin to appear on the surface. Add almond paste, *bhunno*/stir-fry until the fat leaves the sides, add water (approx 1 litre/4¼ cups), bring to a boil, reduce to medium heat, add quails, bring to a boil, reduce to low heat, cover and simmer, stirring occasionally, but carefully, until quails are almost cooked. Uncover, increase to medium heat and cook until the gravy is of medium-thick sauce consistency. Sprinkle green cardamom, cinnamon, clove and mace powders, stir, add saffron, stir, remove and adjust the seasoning.

TO SERVE

Place two quails on each of 4 individual plates, garnish with almond flakes, cover with varq and serve with bread of your choice.

———————— • ————————

BATAER BHARA MURG PASANDA

INGREDIENTS

8 Breasts of Chicken
8 Japanese Quails

Cooking oil to pan grill

The Marination

60ml/¼ cup Lemon Juice
30g/5 tsp Garlic Paste (strain)

15g/2½ tsp Ginger Paste (strain)
Salt

The Stock

1 litre/4¼ cups Chicken Stock

2 *Daalcheeni*/Cinnamon (1" stick)

The Filling

60g/½ cup Bulbs of Spring Onions
12 *Taaza Dhania*/Coriander Stems
5g/½" piece Ginger
2 Green Chillies
7.5g/1 Tbs *Saunf*/Fennel Seeds

24 Black Peppercorns
24 Pistachios
Salt
50g/½ cup Cheese (Cheddar/Processed)

The Gravy

30g/7 tsp *Desi Ghee*/Clarified Butter
5 *Chotti Elaichi*/Green Cardamom
3 *Lavang*/Cloves
2 sticks *Daalcheeni*/Cinnamon (1")
2 *Tej Patta*/Bay Leaf
30g/5 tsp Garlic Paste (strain)
15g/2½ tsp Ginger Paste (strain)

4.5g/1½ tsp *Dhania*/Coriander Powder
1.5g/½ tsp Red Chilli Powder
200g/7 oz *Dahi*/Yoghurt
150g/½ cup Fried Onion Paste
Salt
1g/1/3 tsp Sandalwood Powder
15ml/1 Tbs Lemon Juice

Serves: 4
Preparation Time: 1:45 hours
Cooking Time: 45 minutes

PREPARATION

THE CHICKEN: Clean, remove the skin, bone but retain the winglet bones, wash and pat dry. With a sharp knife, make a deep slit along the thick edge of each breast to make a pocket, taking care not to penetrate the other side.

THE MARINATION: Mix all the ingredients, rub the chicken breasts—inside and out—and reserve for 30 minutes.

THE STOCK: Put stock in a *handi*/stock pot, add the cinnamon, bring to a boil, reduce to low heat and simmer until reduced by a third. Remove and pass through fine muslin into a separate *handi*/pan. Keep aside.

THE FILLING: Clean, bone, wash, pat dry and mince quails. Peel the outer layer, wash and finely chop spring onions. Clean, wash and finely chop coriander stems (use the stems snipped from the accompaniment). Scrape, wash and finely chop ginger. Remove stems, wash, slit, seed and finely chop green chillies. Put fennel and peppercorns in a mortar and crush with a pestle to obtain a coarse powder. Blanch pistachios, cool, remove the skin and halve. Grate cheese in a bowl, add the remaining ingredients, sprinkle salt, mix well and divide into 8 equal portions.

THE STUFFING: Pack a portion of the filling in the pockets of the marinated chicken breasts and then seal each with the tip of a knife, ensuring that meat is not pierced.

THE BRAISING: Heat a little oil in a frying pan, add chicken supremes, two at a time, and braise over medium heat, turning once, until evenly, but lightly, coloured. Remove and keep aside.

THE GRAVY: Whisk yoghurt in a bowl.

COOKING

Heat ghee in a *handi*/pan, add cardamom, cloves, cinnamon and bay leaf, and stir over medium heat until the cardamom begins to change colour. Add the ginger and garlic pastes (dissolved in100ml/7 Tbs of water), *bhunno*/stir-fry until the moisture evaporates, add coriander powder and red chillies (dissolved in 30ml/2 Tbs of water), and *bhunno* /stir-fry until the fat comes to the surface completely and the masala becomes grainy. Then add yoghurt, *bhunno*/stir-fry until the fat leaves the sides, add fried onion paste, *bhunno*/stir-fry until fat leaves the sides, add stock and sprinkle salt, stir and bring to a boil. Now add the braised stuffed chicken, bring to a boil, reduce to low heat and simmer, stirring occasionally, for 7-8 minutes. Remove chicken and keep warm. Pass the gravy through fine muslin into a saucepan, return gravy to heat, add sandalwood, stir, bring to a boil, reduce to low heat and simmer, stirring constantly, until of sauce consistency. Sprinkle lemon juice, stir, remove and adjust the seasoning.

─── • ───

CHOOZA KHAAS MAKHNI

INGREDIENTS

8 Chicken Legs

The First Marination

20g/3½ tsp Garlic Paste (strain)
10g/1¾ tsp Ginger Paste (strain)

60ml/¼ cup Lemon Juice

The Second Marination

110g/½ cup *Dahi*/Yoghurt
30ml/2 Tbs Cream
20g/3½ tsp Garlic Paste (strain)
10g/1¾ tsp Ginger Paste (strain)
3g/1 tsp Red Chilli Powder
1.5g/½ tsp *Jeera*/Cumin Powder
3g/1 tsp *Motti Elaichi*/Black
    Cardamom Powder

1.5g/½ tsp *Chotti Elaichi*/
    Green Cardamom Powder
1.5g/½ tsp *Daalcheeni*/Cinnamon (1")
1.5g/½ tsp *Gulaabpankhrhi*/
    Rose Petal Powder
Salt

The Gravy

90g/3 oz Butter
15g/2½ tsp Ginger paste (strain)
15g/2½ tsp Garlic paste (strain)
1 kg/2¼ lb Tomatoes
10g/1" piece Ginger
2 Green Chillies
20g/3½ tsp Cashewnut Paste

Salt
1.5g/½ tsp Red Chilli Powder
150ml/5 oz Cream
3g/1 tsp *Garam Masala*
1.5g/1 tsp *Kasoori Methi*/
    Dried Fenugreek Leaf Powder

Serves: 4
Preparation Time: 3 hours
Cooking Time: 5-6 minutes

PREPARATION

THE CHICKEN: Clean, wash, bone and cut into 1¼" tikka (cubes).

THE YOGHURT: Whisk in a bowl.

THE MASALA: Put all the spices in a grinder and make a fine powder. Sift and reserve.

THE FIRST MARINATION: Mix all the ingredients and rub the chicken evenly with this marinade. Reserve for 20 minutes.

THE SECOND MARINATION: Whisk yoghurt in a large bowl, add the remaining ingredients and mix well. Rub the chicken with this marinade and reserve for 4 hours in the refrigerator.

THE OVEN: Pre-heat to 350°F.

THE SKEWERING: Skewer the chicken pieces and keep a tray underneath to collect the drippings.

THE VEGETABLES: Remove eyes, wash and roughly chop tomatoes. Scrape, wash and finely chop ginger. Remove stems, wash, slit and seed green chillies.

THE GRILLING: Roast in a moderately hot tandoor for approx 8 minutes, on a charcoal grill for about the same time and in the pre-heated oven for 10 minutes or until 3/4th cooked.

THE GRAVY: Melt half the butter in a *handi*/pan, add the ginger and garlic pastes, stir over medium heat until the moisture evaporates. Then add tomatoes and salt, stir, cover and simmer until tomatoes are mashed. Force the mixture through a fine mesh soup strainer into a separate *handi*/pan and keep aside.

COOKING

Melt the remaining butter in a saucepan, add ginger and green chillies, sauté over medium heat for a minute, add the grilled chicken and stir for a minute. Then add the tomato purée and salt, bring to a boil, reduce to low heat, add cashew nut paste, stir, add red chilli powder and simmer until of thick sauce consistency. Remove, stir-in cream, bring to a boil, sprinkle garam masala and kasoori methi, stir and then adjust the seasoning.

TO SERVE

Dish out equal quantities of the chicken on each of 4 individual plates and serve with Pulao.

MARDAAN MURG MALAAIWALA

INGREDIENTS

8 Breasts of Chicken (bone and
    cut into 3 pieces)
60g/2 oz Onions (finely chop)
10g/1" piece Ginger (finely chop)
4 Green Chillies (seed & finely chop)
960ml/4 cups Milk
360ml/1½ cups Cream
A generous pinch of *Kasoori Methi*/
    Dried Fenugreek Leaf Powder

3g/1 tsp Black Pepper (freshly roasted &
    finely ground)
1.5g/1/2 tsp *Chotti Elaichi*/
    Green Cardamom Powder
0.75g/¼ tsp *Lavang*/Clove Powder
Salt
3g/1 tsp Garam Masala

The Garam Masala

75g/2½ oz *Motti Elaichi*/
    Black Cardamom Seeds
45g/1½ oz *Chotti Elaichi*/Green Cardamom
30g/1 oz *Saunf*/Fennel Seeds
30g/1 oz *Lavang*/Cloves
30g/1 oz *Jeera*/Cumin Seeds
10 sticks *Daalcheeni*/Cinnamon (1")

20g/¾ oz *Javitri*/Mace
20g/¾ oz *Shahi Jeera*/Black Cumin Seeds
15g/½ oz *Tej Patta*/Bay Leaf
15g/½ oz *Gulaabpankhrhi*/Rose Petals
15g/½ oz *Saunth*/Dried Ginger Powder
4 *Jaiphal*/Nutmeg

The Garnish

0.5g/1 tsp *Zaafraan*/Saffron
15ml/1 Tbs Milk

15g/½ oz Almond Flakes

Serves: 4
Preparation Time: 50 minutes (plus time taken to prepare stock)
Cooking Time: 30 minutes

PREPARATION

THE GARAM MASALA : Put all ingredients, except ginger powder, in mortar and pound with pestle to make fine powder. Transfer to clean, dry bowl, add ginger powder and mix well. Sieve and store in sterilized, dry and airtight container.

Yield: Approx 300g/11 oz

THE GARNISH: Reserve saffron and almond flakes in lukewarm milk.

COOKING

Put chicken, onions, ginger, green chillies, 720ml/3 cups of milk, 240ml/1 cup of cream and kasoori methi in a *handi*/pan, and bring to a boil over medium heat, stirring constantly. Once it comes to a boil, reduce to low heat, cover and simmer, stirring at regular intervals until the chicken is almost cooked and the milk and cream are absorbed. Uncover, add the remaining ingredients, including milk and cream, bring to just under a boil, remove and adjust the seasoning.

TO SERVE

Remove to a service dish, garnish with saffron threads and almond flakes, and serve warm with Naan or Kulcha.

———————————— • ————————————

MURG KIBTI

INGREDIENTS

1 Kg/2¼ lb Chicken *Tikka* (from the thigh)
400ml/1¾ cups *Dahi*/Yoghurt (whisk)
75g/6 Tbs *Desi Ghee*/Clarified Butter
500g/1 lb 2 oz Onions (slice)
30g/5¼ tsp Garlic Paste (strain)
20g/3½ tsp Ginger Paste (strain)
12g/4 tsp *Dhania*/Coriander Powder
6g/2 tsp *Kashmiri Deghi Mirch* Powder

3g/1 tsp *Haldee*/Turmeric Powder
8 *Chotti Elaichi*/Green Cardamoms
4 *Lavang*/Cloves
0.75g/ ¼ tsp *Javitri*/Mace Powder
12 Black Peppercorns
Salt
1g/2 tsp *Zaafraan*/Saffron
30ml/2 Tbs Water

The Garnish

15g/½ oz Toasted Almond Flakes

3.25g/1 Tbs *Taaza Dhania*/Coriander (chop)

Serves: 4
Preparation Time: 1:30 hours
Cooking Time: 25 minutes

PREPARATION

THE MARINATION: Crush saffron threads with a pestle or the back of a spoon, soak in lukewarm water and then make a paste. Mix with the ingredients in a large bowl, evenly rub the chicken with this marinade and reserve in the bowl for one hour.

COOKING

Put the chicken, along with the marinade, in a *handi*/pan, and bring to a boil, stirring constantly, over medium heat. Reduce to low heat, cover and simmer, stirring at regular intervals, until the chicken is almost cooked. Uncover, increase to medium heat, and *bhunno*/stir-fry until specks of fat appear on the surface, chicken is cooked and gravy is of coating consistency. Remove and adjust the seasoning.

TO SERVE

Remove to a service dish, garnish with almond flakes and fresh coriander and serve with bread of your choice.

———————— • ————————

MURG KALIMIRCH

INGREDIENTS

1kg Chicken *Tikka* (boneless thigh cut into 1½" cubes
2 *Laal Shimla Mirch*/Red Bell Peppers (¼" thick strips)

2 *Peeli Shimla Mirch*/Yellow Bell Peppers (¼" thick strips)
60g/2 oz *Harra Pyaaz*/Spring Onion Greens (1½" long thin strips)

The Chicken Marination

15ml/1 Tbs Lemon Juice
25g/4 tsp Garlic Paste (strain)
15g/2½ tsp Ginger Paste (strain)

8g/2 tsp Black Peppercorns (crush)
Salt

The Masala

45ml/3 Tbs Cooking Oil (preferably mustard)
250g/9 oz Onions (chop)
15g/2½ tsp Garlic Paste (strain)

Salt
0.5g/1 tsp *Kasoori Methi* (crush between palms before sprinkling)

10g/1¾ tsp Ginger Paste (strain)
120ml/½ cup Tomato Purée (canned)
4g/2 tsp *Dhania*/Coriander Seeds (crushed)
3g/1 tsp Red Chilli Powder
Salt
120ml/½ cup Chicken Stock (or water)
15ml/1 Tbs Lemon Juice
6g/1Tbs *Arraroot*/Cornflour
3.25g/1 Tbs *Dhania*/Coriander (chop)

20g/1¾ tsp Black Pepper Powder
  (coarsely ground)
A pinch *Kaala Namak*/Black Rock Salt
A pinch *Daalcheeni*/Cinnamon Powder
A pinch *Lavang*/Clove Powder
A pinch *Chotti Elaichi*/
  Green Cardamom Powder
A pinch *Javitri*/Mace Powder
1 tsp *Sua*/Soya/Dill

Serves: 4
Preparation Time: 45 minutes
Cooking Time: 15 minutes

PREPARATION

THE CHICKEN MARINATION: Mix all the ingredients in a bowl, rub the chicken with the marinade and reserve in the bowl itself for 15 minutes.

COOKING

Heat oil in a *kadhai*/wok, add onions, sauté over medium heat until translucent and glossy, add the garlic and ginger pastes, sauté until the onions are light golden, add tomato purée, coriander and red chilli powders, *bhunno*/stir-fry until the moisture evaporates. Then add the marinated chicken, increase to high heat, *bhunno*/stir-fry for 2 minutes, add the bell peppers and spring onions, *bhunno*/stir-fry for a minute, add the stock (or water), stir, add lemon juice, coriander and salt, stir. Cook for another five minutes. Now, add cornflour-dissolved in 45ml/3 Tbs of water, and stir until the moisture has almost evaporated. Sprinkle the powdered spices, stir, remove and adjust the seasoning.

TO SERVE

Remove to a platter, garnish with dill and serve with Tandoori Roti, Phulka, or Roomali Roti.

PESHAWARI TALLE MURGE

INGREDIENTS

16 *Tangrhi*/Chicken Drumsticks
   (large & juicy)
Sarson/Mustard Oil to deep fry
60g/2 oz *Maida*/Flour
60g/2 oz *Besan*/Gramflour
30g/1 oz *Arraroot*/Cornflour
2 Eggs
20g/3¼ tsp Garlic Paste (strain)
15g/2½ tsp Ginger Paste (strain)
1g/1/2 tsp *Ajwain*/Carom Seeds
3g/1 tsp *Kashmiri Deghi Mirch* Powder

4.5g/1½ tsp *Jeera*/Cumin Powder
1.5g/½ tsp *Motti Elaichi*/
   Black Cardamom Powder
0.75g/¼ tsp *Lavang*/Cloves Powder
0.75g/¼ tsp *Maghay* Powder
   (or *Daalcheeni*/Cinnamon Powder)
0.375g/1/8 tsp *Jaiphal*/Nutmeg Powder
Salt
2 Green Chillies (seed & chop)
10ml/2 tsp Lemon Juice

Serves: 4
Preparation Time: 3:15 hours
Cooking Time: 4-5 minutes per set

PREPARATION

THE BATTER: Beat eggs in a bowl, add the remaining ingredients and enough water to make a batter of fritter (*pakorha*) consistency.

COOKING

Heat oil in a *kadhai*/wok to a smoking point over medium heat, remove and cool. Re-heat oil, add a few drops of the batter, as soon as the batter droplets come to the surface, dip the chicken drumsticks in the batter and deep fry until crisp and golden. Remove to absorbent paper to drain the excess fat.

TO SERVE

Arrange doiley paper on a service platter, place the pakorha on top and serve with mint chutney.

LIBERHAYA MURG

INGREDIENTS

1Kg/2¼ lb *Dasti*/ Breast of Chicken
(boned 1½" cubes)
200g/1cup *Desi Ghee*/Clarified Butter
12g/2Tbs *Dhania*/ Coriander Seeds
(pound gently to split)
60g/2 oz Brown Cashew nut Paste
120ml/ ½ cup Tomato Purée
220g/ ½ lb Tomato (chopped)
3g/1tsp Cumin Seeds
50g/3Tbs Garlic (chopped fine)
20g/3¼Tbsp Ginger Paste
390g/3cups Onion (chopped)
120ml/½ cup *Dahi*/ Yoghurt (whisked)

6g/2tsp *Kashmiri Deghi Mirch*/
Kashmiri Chilli Powder
1.5g/½ tsp *Chotti Elaichi*/
Green Cardamom Powder
1.5 g/½ tsp *Shahi Jeera*/
Black Cumin Powder
0.375g/1/8 tsp *Daalcheeni*/
Cinnamon Powder
0.375g/1/8 tsp *Lavang*/Clove Powder
Salt
475ml/2 cup Chicken Stock
6.5g/2 Tbs *Taaza Dhania*/ Coriander
leaves (chopped fine)

Serves: 4
Preparation Time: 1:15 hours
Cooking Time: 55 minutes

COOKING

Heat ghee in a *handi* / pan, add cumin seeds and stir over medium heat until they begin to pop, add garlic and sauté till light golden. Add the chopped onion and *bhunno*/stir-fry till golden brown. Sprinkle the crushed coriander and add the chopped ginger. Sauté for a minute, add the red chilli powder and stir till the fat leaves the side of the pan. Now, add the chopped tomatoes and cook on medium heat stirring occasionally till cooked. Whisk the yoghurt in a bowl and pour on to the pan, and sauté for a couple of minutes. Add the tomato purée and *bhunno*/ stir-fry till the fat leaves the side. Slowly stir in the brown cashew nut paste and simmer for 2 minutes. Then add the chicken, increase to high heat and bring to boil. Reduce to low heat, cover and simmer, stirring at regular intervals and adding warm chicken stock as required. Uncover, increase to medium heat and *bhunno*/ stir-fry till specks of fat appear on the surface, and the chicken is cooked. Sprinkle the cardamom, clove, black cumin and cinnamon powders and adjust the seasoning.

TO SERVE

Arrange in a serving bowl and serve hot, garnished with chopped fresh coriander leaves.

———————— • ————————

METHI MURG

INGREDIENTS

8 Breasts of Chicken
4 Chicken Drumsticks
400g *Methi*/Fenugreek
45ml/3 tbsp Cooking Oil
12g/1tbsp *Desi Ghee*/Clarified Butter
5 *Chhoti Elaichi*/Green Cardamom
2 *Motti Elaichi*/Black Cardamom
10 *Lavang*/Cloves
2 Sticks *Daalcheeni*/Cinnamon (1-inch)

2 *Tej Patta*/Bay Leaves
150g/5½ oz Onion
25g/4tsp Garlic Paste
15g/2½tsp Ginger Paste
100g Tomato Paste (fresh or canned)
Salt
200g *Dahi*/Yoghurt
1g *Javitri*/Mace Powder

The Garnish

4 Green Chillies
10g Ginger
1 Tomato

10g/3Tbsp *Taaza Dhania*/
    Fresh Coriander (chopped fine)

Serves: 4
Preparation Time: 45 minutes
Cooking Time: 25 minutes

PREPARATION

THE CHICKEN: Clean, trim, wash and pat dry.

THE FENUGREEK: Clean, wash and finely chop. Sprinkle salt, keep aside for 5-7 minutes. Then squeeze in a napkin to drain the moisture.

THE ONIONS: Peel, wash and finely chop.

THE YOGHURT: Whisk in a bowl.

THE GARNISH: Remove stems, slit, deseed and wash green chillies. Scrape, wash and cut ginger into juliennes. Remove eyes and blanch tomatoes, halve, remove the pulp and cut into thin strips.

COOKING

Heat oil in a *handi*/pan, add green cardamom, black cardamom, cloves, cinnamon and bay leaves, stir over medium heat until the green cardamon is light golden. Remove the spices with a strainer. Then add onions, sauté until golden brown, add the ginger and garlic pastes—both dissolved in 30ml of water—and *bhunno*/stir-fry for 3-4 minutes, adding a little water if it threatens to stick to the bottom of the handi. Add chicken, stir, sprinkle turmeric and salt, stir and then *bhunno*/stir-fry fo 5 minutes, add water (approx 180 ml), bring to a boil, reduce to low heat, cover and simmer, stirring occasionally, until the chicken is cooked. Uncover and cook, stirring occasionally, until the liquid evaporates. Now add tomato purée, stir and cook, stirring occasionally for 3-4, minutes, add fenugreek, and *bhunno*/stir-fry for 10 minutes (if using refreshed fenugreek, for 4-5 minutes). Remove *handi* from heat, stir-in yoghurt, return *handi* to heat, cover and simmer, with fenugreek. Remove and adjust the seasoning.

TO SERVE

Remove to a platter, garnish with green chillies, ginger and tomato strips, serve with Phulka or Tandoori Roti.

* If fresh fenugreek is not available refresh 250g of dried fenugreek leaves in water for 15 - 20 minutes and then drain and chop. Add 100g of cleaned, washed and finely chopped spinach.

— • —

KHEEMA KALEJI te ANDEY

INGREDIENTS

400g/ 14 oz Lamb Liver
400g/ 14 oz Lamb Mince
2g/ 2/3 tsp *Haldi*/ Turmeric Powder
Salt
100g/½ cup *Desi Ghee*/Clarified Butter
200g/ 1¼ cup Onions
4 Green Chillies

10g/1Tbsp Ginger
4 Whole Red Chillies
5g/2½ tsp *Dhania*/Coriander Seeds
60ml/¼ cup Lemon Juice
20g/¹⁄₃ cup *Dhania*/Coriander Leaves
10g/2tsp Garam Masala

The Kadhai Gravy

35g/3Tbsp *Desi Ghee*/ Clarified Butter
15g/2½ tsp Garlic Paste
4 Whole Red Chillies
1 Green Chilli (seeded and chopped fine)
20g/ 3¼ tsp Ginger (chopped fine)

350g/1½ cup Tomatoes (roughly chopped)
5g/1tbsp *Kasoori Methi*/ Dried
 Fenugreek Leaves
Salt
5g/1 tsp *Garam Masala*

Serves:4
Preparation Time: 55 minutes (plus 35 minutes for *kadhai* gravy)
Cooking Time: 12-13 minutes

PREPARATION

THE LIVER: Clean, wash and pat dry. Put turmeric, salt and water in a *handi* and bring to a boil. Add the liver and boil for couple of minutes. Drain and dice the liver.

THE VEGETABLES: Peel, wash and chop onions. Remove stems, wash, slit, deseed and chop green chillies. Scrape wash and chop ginger. Clean, wash and chop coriander.

THE WHOLE SPICES: Pound red chillies and coriander seeds with a pestle.

COOKING
The Kadhai Gravy

Heat ghee in a *kadhai*, add garlic paste and sauté over medium heat until light brown. Add the pounded spices, sauté for 30 seconds, add green chillies and ginger, sauté for 30 seconds. Then add tomatoes and *bhunno*/stir-fry until the fat comes to the surface. Now add fenugreek and salt, stir. Sprinkle garam masala and stir.

The Liver and Mince

Heat ghee on a large *tawa*, add onions, green chillies and ginger, sauté over medium heat for 3 minutes. Add the pounded spices, stir for 30 seconds, add the mince and *bhunno*/stir-fry for 5 minutes, stirring constantly. Now transfer the liver to the *tawa* and roughly chop the mixture with two metal spatulae held vertically. For the following 2-3 minutes, stir and fold the mixture. Then add the *kadhai* gravy and lemon juice and *bhunno*/stir-fry until the gravy becomes thick. Adjust the seasoning.

Sprinkle garam masala and chopped coriander, stir.

TO SERVE

Remove to a dish and serve with an Indian bread of your choice.

———————— • ————————

MUTTAR NUKTA

INGREDIENTS

800g/1 lb 11 oz *Dasti*/Shoulder of Kid/
   Lamb (boned 1½" cubes)
250g/9 oz Green Peas
75g/6 Tbs *Desi Ghee*/Clarified Butter
350g/13 oz Onions (chop)
30g/5¼ tsp Garlic Paste (strain)
20g/3½ tsp Ginger Paste (strain)
15g/5 tsp *Dhania*/Coriander Powder
4.5g/1½ tsp Red Chilli Powder
3g/1 tsp *Haldee*/Turmeric Powder
Salt
250ml/1 cup *Dahi*/Yoghurt (whisk)

240ml/1 cup Fresh Tomato Purée
30g/1 oz Almond Paste
1.5g/½ tsp *Chotti Elaichi*/
   Green Cardamom Powder
0.75g/¼ tsp *Motti Elaichi*/
   Green Cardamom Powder
0.75g/¼ tsp *Lavang*/Clove Powder
0.375g/⅛ tsp *Daalcheeni*/
   Cinnamon Powder
0.375g/⅛ tsp *Javitri*/Mace Powder
6.5g/2 Tbs *Taaza Dhania*/Coriander (chop)
10g/1" piece Ginger (cut into juliennes)

Serves: 4
Preparation Time: 45 minutes
Cooking Time: 1:15 hours

COOKING

Heat ghee in a *handi*/pan, add onions, sauté over medium heat until light golden, add the garlic and ginger pastes, sauté until onions are golden, add coriander, red chilli and turmeric powders (dissolved in 60ml/¼ cup of water) and *bhunno*/stir-fry until the moisture evaporates. Then add meat, increase to high heat and *bhunno*/stir-fry to sear for 2 minutes. Reduce to low heat, add salt, stir, cover and simmer, stirring at regular intervals, for 20 minutes (adding water in small quantities at regular intervals to prevent sticking). Uncover, increase to medium heat, and *bhunno*/stir-fry until the moisture evaporates. Remove *handi*/pan from heat, stir-in yoghurt, return *handi*/pan to heat, and *bhunno*/stir-fry until the fat leaves the sides. Now add tomatoes, almond paste and peas, *bhunno*/stir-fry until the fat leaves, add water (approx 480ml/2 cups) and cook, stirring occasionally, until the meat and peas are napped. Remove, sprinkle green cardamom, black cardamom, cloves, cinnamon and mace, stir and adjust the seasoning.

TO SERVE

Remove to a service dish, garnish with fresh coriander and ginger, and serve with bread of your choice.

———————— • ————————

SAAGWALA MEAT

INGREDIENTS

750g/1lb 11 oz *Dasti*/Shoulder of
   Kid/Lamb (1½" boned cubes)
650g/1lb 9 oz Spinach (chop)
150g/5 oz *Methi*/Fresh Fenugreek (chop)
100g/½ cup *Desi Ghee*/Clarified Butter
5 *Chotti Elaichi*/Green Cardamom
4 *Lavang*/Cloves
3 *Motti Elaichi*/Black Cardamom
2 sticks *Daalcheeni*/Cinnamon (1")
2 *Tej Patta*/Bay Leaf
300g/11 oz Onions (chop)
12 flakes Garlic (chop)
15g/1½" piece Ginger (chop)

4 Green Chillies (seed and chop)
3g/1 tsp Red Chilli Powder
3g/1 tsp *Haldee*/Turmeric Powder
Salt
150g/5 oz Tomato (chop)
4.5g/1½ tsp *Jeera*/Cumin Powder
   (freshly roasted)
A generous pinch *Kasoori Methi*/
   Fenugreek Powder
10g/1" piece Ginger (juliennes; reserved in
   15ml/1 Tbs Lemon Juice)
30ml/1oz Cream

Serves: 4
Preparation Time: 45 minutes
Cooking Time: 1:15 hours

COOKING

Heat ghee in a *kadhai*/wok, add green cardamom, cloves, black cardamom, cinnamon and bay leaf, and stir over medium heat until the green cardamom begins to change colour. Add onions, garlic, and sauté until onions are light golden, add ginger and green chillies, stir for a few seconds, add meat, increase to high heat and sear for 2-3 minutes. Reduce to medium heat, add red chillies, turmeric and salt, and stir for a few seconds. Reduce to low heat, cover and simmer, until the meat releases all its juices. Uncover and *bhunno*/stir-fry until the moisture evaporates. Add tomatoes and *bhunno*/stir-fry until fat leaves the sides and the meat is almost cooked. Now add spinach and fresh fenugreek, and *bhunno*/stir-fry until the meat is cooked, the liquid has evaporated and the spinach and fenugreek nappe the meat. Stir in the cream and simmer for a minute. Sprinkle cumin and kasoori methi, stir, remove and adjust the seasoning.

TO SERVE

Remove to a service dish, garnish with ginger juliennes and serve with Phulka, Roomali Roti or Tandoori Roti.

———————— • ————————

BHUNA ALOO TAMATER te MEAT

INGREDIENTS

800g/1 lb 13 oz *Dasti*/Shoulder of Kid/ Lamb (1½" boned cubes)

16 Baby Potatoes (or parisiennes*)

The Marination

60g/2 oz *Chakka Dahi*/Yoghurt Cheese (hung yoghurt)
25g/4 tsp Garlic Paste (strain)
15g/2½ tsp Ginger Paste (strain)

15g/1¾ tsp Green Chilli Paste
Salt
30ml/2 Tbs Lemon Juice

The Masala

45ml/3 Tbs Mustard Oil
3 Red Chillies
1.5g/½ tsp Black Peppercorn
1g/½ tsp *Jeera*/Cumin Seeds
10g/1¾ tsp Garlic Paste (strain)
10g/1¾ tsp Ginger Paste (strain)
4.5g/1½ tsp *Dhania*/Coriander Powder
3g/1 tsp Red Chilli Powder
1.5g/½ tsp *Haldee*/Turmeric Powder
150g/5 oz *Harra Pyaaz*/Spring Onions
Salt
120ml/½ cup Chicken Stock (or water)

16 Cherry Tomatoes
15ml/1 Tbs Lemon Juice
6.5g/2 Tbs *Dhania*/Coriander (chop)
4g/2 Tbs *Pudhina*/Mint (chop)
A generous pinch *Amchoor*/Mango Powder
A generous pinch Black Pepper Powder (coarsely ground)
A pinch *Kaala Namak*/Black Rock Salt
A pinch *Chakriphool*/Star Anise Powder
A pinch *Chotti Elaichi*/Green Cardamom Powder
A pinch *Javitri*/Mace Powder

The Garnish

4 Pickled Green Chillies (juliennes)

Serves: 4
Preparation Time: 45 minutes
Cooking Time: 10-12 minutes

PREPARATION

THE LAMB MARINATION: Whisk yoghurt cheese in a bowl, add the remaining ingredients, rub the tikka with the marinade and reserve in the bowl itself for 30 minutes.

THE POTATOES: Boil in salted water until al dente (almost cooked). Do not remove the skin. (*If baby potatoes are not available, scoop parisiennes from large peeled potatoes and then boil until al dente). Drain and keep aside.

THE SPRING ONIONS: Cut the bulbs (whites) into roundels and separate the rings. Cut the green into 1½" long thin strips.

COOKING

Heat oil in a large *kadhai*/wok, add cumin seeds, stir over medium heat until they begin to pop, add red chilli whole, and stir. Add garlic and ginger pastes, stir, add coriander, red chilli and turmeric powders, dissolved in 60ml/¼ cup of water, and *bhunno*/stir-fry until the specks of fat begin to appear on the surface. Then add onion rings, stir, add the marinated lamb and salt, lower the heat, simmer covered for 12-13 minutes, add potatoes and stock (or water), stir until the lamb is cooked. Now add cherry tomatoes, spring onion greens, lemon juice, coriander and mint, stir until the moisture has almost evaporated. Sprinkle the powdered spices, stir, remove and adjust the seasoning.

TO SERVE

Remove to a platter, garnish with pickled green chillies and serve with Tandoori Roti, Phulka, or Roomali Roti.

———————— • ————————

NALLIWALA MEAT

INGREDIENTS

12 Kid/Lamb *Nalli*/Shanks	10g/1¾ tsp Ginger Paste (strain)
90g/7 Tbs *Desi Ghee*/Clarified Butter	4.5g/1½ tsp *Dhania*/Coriander Powder
6 *Motti Elaichi*/Black Cardamom	4.5g/1½ tsp Red Chilli Powder

6 *Chotti Elaichi*/Green Cardamom Powder
5 *Lavang*/Cloves
3 sticks *Daalcheeni*/Cinnamon (1")
3 *Tej Patta*/Bay Leaf
6g/1 Tbs *Jeera*/Cumin Seeds
200g/7 oz Onions
30g/5 tsp Garlic Paste (strain)

30g/2 Tbs *Khus-khus*/Poppy Seed Paste
125g/½ cup Fresh Tomato Purée
3g/1 tsp *Chotti Elaichi*/
     Green Cardamom Powder
15ml/1Tbsp Lemon Juice
Salt
Cooking Oil to grease roasting tray

The Marination

250g/1 cup *Dahi*/Yoghurt
30g/5 tsp Garlic Paste (strain)
15g/2½ tsp Ginger Paste (strain)

1g/¹⁄₃ tsp *Jaiphal*/Nutmeg (freshly grated)
Salt

The Stock

1.5 litres/6½ cups Kid/Lamb Stock

15g/½ oz *Taaza Pudhina*/Mint

The Garnish

10g/1" piece Ginger
4 sprigs Coriander

15ml/1 Tbs Lemon Juice

Serves: 4
Preparation Time: 3:30 hours
Cooking Time: 1:45 hours

PREPARATION

THE KID/LAMB: Clean the nalli, remove the sinews, wash and pat dry. (Ask the butcher for nalli, ensuring they are open-ended on both sides.) Then remove the meat by carefully scraping along the length of 4 nalli starting at the narrower end, to expose the bone, leaving an inch from the other end. (This is done so that when the meat is braised, it shrivels at the unexposed end, making the nalli easy to cut at the time of eating. Also, it makes the dish more attractive.) In the case of the remaining 8 nalli, scrape along the entire length of the bone and remove the meat completely. Reserve the bones for the stock.

THE VEGETABLES: Peel, wash and slice onions.

THE MARINATION: Whisk yoghurt in a large bowl, add the remaining ingredients and mix well. Rub the nalli and the boneless meat with this marinade and reserve for 3 hours.

THE STOCK: Clean, wash and pluck the mint leaves. Put stock in a *handi*/pan bring to a boil, add mint and the *khus*, reduce to low heat and simmer for 3-4 minutes. Remove, pass the stock through a fine mesh sieve into a separate *handi*/pan and keep aside.

THE GARNISH: Scrape, wash, cut ginger into fine juliennes, reserve in lemon juice and drain at the time of plating (they should be of a pink hue). Clean and wash coriander.

THE OVEN: Pre-heat to 250°F.

COOKING

Heat ghee to a smoking point in a *handi*/pan reduce to medium heat, add the black cardamom, green cardamom, cloves, cinnamon, bay leaf and cumin, and stir until green cardamom begins to change colour. Then add onions, sauté until light brown, add the ginger and garlic pastes, sauté until onions are golden brown. Remove nalli and the boneless meat from the marinade, add to the masala, increase to high heat and *bhunno*/stir-fry for three minutes. Reduce to low heat; cover and cook, stirring occasionally, for 20 minutes (add a little stock to prevent sticking, if necessary). Uncover, *bhunno*/stir-fry until the liquid has evaporated, add coriander powder and one-fourth of the marinade, and *bhunno*/stir-fry until the liquid has evaporated. Add another fourth of the marinade and keep repeating the process until the marinade is used up. Now add red chillies (dissolved in 30ml/ 2 Tbs of water), stir for a minute, add poppy seed paste, stir, reduce to low heat, and *bhunno*/stir-fry until the fat leaves the sides. Add tomato purée, *bhunno*/ stir-fry until the fat leaves the sides again, add the stock, bring to a boil, reduce to low heat, cover and simmer, stirring occasionally, until the nalli and the boneless meat are cooked. Uncover, remove the nalli and the boneless meat, keep aside. Pass the gravy through fine muslin into a separate *handi*/pan, return gravy to heat, add lemon juice and reduce over low heat to sauce consistency. Remove and adjust the seasoning. Sprinkle cardamom powder, stir, and keep warm.

TO SERVE

Put nalli (shanks) and the boneless meat in a greased roasting tray, put the tray in the pre-heated oven and roast under top heat, turning to ensure the meat is evenly coloured. Place a nalli (shank) in the middle of each of four individual plates, and arrange an equal quantity of the boneless meat around it. Pour on equal quantities of the gravy, sprinkle ginger juliennes on the meat, arrange the coriander sprigs on top of the meat and serve warm.

KHUBANIANWALA MEAT

INGREDIENTS

1 Kg/2¼ lb *Boti*/Leg of Kid/
   Lamb (boned 1½" chunks)
16 *Khubani*/Dried Apricots
75g/2½ oz *Desi Ghee*/Clarified Butter
6 *Chotti Elaichi*/Green Cardamom
4 *Lavang*/Cloves
300g/11 oz Onions (thin slices)
30g/5 tsp Garlic Paste (strain)

15g/2½ tsp Ginger Paste (strain)
30g/2 Tbs *Khus-khus*/Poppy Seed Paste
90ml/3 oz Fresh Tomato Purée
3g/1 tsp *Chotti Elaichi*/
   Green Cardamom Powder
1g/2 tsp *Zaafraan*/Saffron
Cooking Oil to grease roasting tray

The Marination

250g/1 cup *Dahi*/Yoghurt
4.5g/1½ tsp *Dhania*/Coriander Powder
4.5g/1½ tsp Red Chilli Powder

3g/1 tsp *Haldee*/Turmeric Powder
24 'Black Peppercorns
Salt

The Stock

1 litre/4¼ cups Kid/Lamb Stock

5g/1½ tsp *Khada Garam Masala*/
   Whole Spices

The Garnish

15g/½ oz Toasted Almond Flakes

4 sprigs *Taaza Dhania*/Coriander

Serves: 4
Preparation Time: 3:30 hours
Cooking Time: 1:45 hours

PREPARATION

THE APRICOTS: Wash thoroughly, drain, soak in 240ml/1 cup of lukewarm water until plump (approx 30 minutes), remove the apricots, pass the liquid through fine muslin and reserve.

 THE MARINATION: Whisk yoghurt in a large bowl, add the remaining ingredients and mix well. Rub the meat with this marinade and reserve for 3 hours

THE STOCK: Put kid/lamb stock in a *handi*/pan bring to a boil, add khada garam masala, reduce to low heat and simmer for 10-12 minutes. Remove, pass the stock through a fine mesh sieve into a separate *handi*/pan and keep aside.

THE SAFFRON: Crush the threads with a pestle or the back of a spoon, reserve in 15ml/1 Tbs of lukewarm water for 15 minutes and then grind into a paste.

COOKING

Heat ghee in a *handi*/pan, add cardamom and cloves, stir over medium heat until cardamom begins to change colour, add onions, sauté until translucent and glossy, add the ginger and garlic pastes, sauté until onions are light golden. Then add the meat, along with the marinade, *bhunno*/stir-fry until the liquor begins to boil. Reduce to low heat, cover and simmer, stirring occasionally, until the meat is three-fourths cooked (add a little stock to prevent sticking, as and when necessary). Uncover, *bhunno*/stir-fry until the liquid has evaporated, add poppy seed paste, stir, *bhunno*/stir-fry until the fat leaves the sides, add tomato purée and *bhunno*/stir-fry until the fat leaves the sides. Now add the stock, bring to a boil, reduce to low heat, add apricots and the reserved liquor, cover and simmer, stirring occasionally, until the meat is cooked and the gravy is of thin sauce consistency. Remove and adjust the seasoning. Now add cardamom powder and saffron, stir and keep warm.

TO SERVE

Remove to a bowl, garnish with almonds and coriander and serve with Phulka, Naan, Tandoori Roti or Steamed Rice.

MAGAZ MASALA

INGREDIENTS

8 Kid/Lamb Brains
480ml/2 cups Milk
45ml/3 Tbs Brandy
3g/1 tsp *Haldee*/Turmeric Powder
4 *Motti Elaichi*/Black Cardamoms
4 *Lavang*/Cloves
  2 sticks *Daalcheeni*/Cinnamon (1")
3 *Tej Patta*/Bay Leaf

10g/1¾ tsp Garlic Paste (strain)
450ml/2 cups *Dhania*/Coriander Powder
6g/2 tsp Red Chilli Powder
1.5g/½ tsp *Haldee*/Turmeric Powder
30g/1 oz Cashew nut Paste
1.5g/½ tsp *Chotti Elaichi*/
  Green Cardamom Powder
1.5 g/½ tsp *Shahi Jeera*/Black Cumin Powder

75g/6Tbs *Desi Ghee*/ Clarified Butter
2g/1 tsp *Jeera*/Cumin Seeds
1.5g/1tsp *Methidaana*/Fenugreek Seeds
3g/2tsp *Saunf*/Fennel Powder
250g/9 oz Onions
20g/3¼ tsp Ginger Paste (strain)

0.375g/⅛ tsp *Daalcheeni*/
   Cinnamon Powder
0.375g/⅛ tsp *Lavang*/Clove Powder
Salt
10ml/2 tsp Lemon Juice

The Garnish

2 Green Chillies
3.25g/1 Tbs *Dhania*/Coriander

Ginger juliennes

Serves: 4
Preparation Time: 3:15 hours
Cooking Time: 15 minutes

PREPARATION

THE BRAIN: Clean, remove the sinews, wash, pat dry, put in a panful of milk, add brandy and reserve overnight in the refrigerator. Put the remaining ingredients in a panful of water, bring to a boil, drain and add brain, and boil for 2 minutes. Remove and keep aside.

THE ONIONS: Peel, wash and finely chop.

THE YOGHURT MIXTURE: Whisk in a bowl, add coriander, red chilli and turmeric powders, whisk to homogenise.

THE GARNISH: Wash green chillies, slit, seed, cut into juliennes and discard the stems. Clean, wash, and finely chop coriander.

COOKING

Spread ghee on a *handi*/pan, add garlic, sauté over medium heat with a spatula until light golden, add onions and sauté until onions become translucent and glossy. Add ginger and green chillies, stir for a few seconds, add the yoghurt mixture, *bhunno*/stir-fry until the fat leaves the sides. Now add the cashew nut paste and *bhunno*/stir-fry until the fat leaves the side. Then add 480ml/ 2 cups of water, bring to a boil, reduce to low heat, sprinkle green cardamom, black cumin, cinnamon, clove, fennel and powders, stir, add salt, stir, cover with a lid and cook on *dum* for 20 minutes. Then add the cooked brain and *bhunno*/stir-fry, simultaneously 'chopping' the brain with the spatula into ¾" pieces, until the masala nappes the brain. Now add coriander and stir, turning with the spatula to incorporate. Remove, sprinkle lemon juice, stir, and adjust the seasoning.

TO SERVE

Remove to a flat dish, garnish with green chillies, coriander and ginger juliennes, serve with Paratha.

————————————— • —————————————

RAAN HARI SINGH NALWA

INGREDIENTS

2 Leg of Kid/Lamb (approx 3 lb/1.3 Kg)
5 *Chotti Elaichi*/Green Cardamom
3 *Motti Elaichi*/Black Cardamom
3 *Lavang*/Cloves

2 *Tej Patta*/Bay Leaf
2 stick *Daalcheeni*/Cinnamon (1")
Butter to baste

The Marination

Salt
4 tsp/12g Red Chilli Powder
7 tsp/40g Garlic Paste (strain)

¼ cup/60ml *Sirka*/Malt Vinegar
3½ tsp/20g Ginger Paste (strain)

Serves: 4
Preparation: 4:30 hours
Cooking: 6-7minutes

PREPARATION

THE KID/LAMB LEG: Clean, remove the blade bone and then, using boning knife, loosen meat around thighbone (do not expose bone, merely loosen meat). Wash and pat dry.

THE MARINATION: Forcefully rub—as in massage—kid/lamb leg, inside and out, with salt. Repeat process with red chillies, garlic paste, ginger paste and vinegar. (Remember, each of these ingredients is to be rubbed separately and not as mixture). Refrigerate for 4 hours.

THE OVEN: Pre-heat to 350 °F.

THE BRAISING: Arrange kid/lamb leg in roasting pan (pan should be just about large enough for leg), add green and black cardamom, cloves, bay leaves, cinnamon and just enough water to cover legs. Then cover pan loosely with lid or foil (it shouldn't be sealed or air-tight), braise in pre-heated oven for an hour, reduce oven temperature (to 275 °F) and continue to braise until meat is tender and leaves bones from ends, and the liquor is almost absorbed.

SKEWERING: Skewer right down middle, horizontally, and as close to bone as possible. For the oven, arrange the legs on a greased roasting tray and baste with butter.

COOKING

Roast in a moderately hot tandoor for 4 minutes, remove, hang the skewers to allow the excess moisture to drip off, baste with butter and roast again for 2 minutes. Arrange the legs on a pre-heated charcoal grill and roast over medium heat, turning and basting at regular intervals, for 6-7 minutes. Place the tray in the pre-heated oven and roast, turning and basting with butter and the drippings twice, for 6-7 minutes or until cooked and coloured.

———————————— • ————————————

TARRIWALA MEAT

INGREDIENTS

1kg/2¼ lb Leg of Mutton
100g/½ cup *Desi Ghee*/Calrified Butter
3 *Chhoti Elaichi*/Green Cardamom
2 *Motti Elaichi*/Black Cardamom
3 sticks *Daalcheeni*/Cinnamon (1-inch)
2 *Tej Patta*/Bay Leaves
250g/1 cup Onion Paste (raw)
10g/1½ tsp Ginger Paste
10g/1¾ tsp Garlic Paste

6g/2 tsp *Jeera*/Cumin Seeds
5g/¾ tsp Red Chilli Paste
5g/1 tsp *Dhania*/Coriander Powder
2g/¼ tsp *Haldee*/Turmeric
Salt
350g/1½ cups Tomatoes (roughly chop)
110g/2/3 cup Onions (roughly chop)
60g/1 cup *Taaza Dhania*/Coriander
2g/¼ tsp *Garam Masala*

Serves: 4
Preparation Time: 45 minutes
Cooking Time: 1:30 hours

PREPARATION

THE MUTTON: Clean, wash and cut into 1½" chunks.
THE CORIANDER: Clean, wash and roughly chop 45g/¾ cup of coriander, finely chop the rest for garnish.

COOKING

Heat ghee in a *handi*/pan, add green cardamom, black cardamom, cinnamon and bay leaves, sauté until the whole spices begin to crackle, add onion paste, sauté until transparent (make sure that the onions do not get coloured) add the ginger and garlic pastes, stir for 30 seconds, add cumin seeds and stir. Then add red chilli paste, coriander powder, turmeric and salt, all dissolved in 60ml/¼ cup of water, *bhunno*/stir-fry until the fat leaves the masala, add the mutton chunks, *bhunno* until the fat leaves the masala again, add tomatoes and *bhunno*/stir-fry until the fat leaves the masala a third time. Now add onions and water (approx 2 litres/8⅓ cups), bring to a boil, cover and simmer, stirring occasionally, until mutton is almost cooked, add the roughly chopped coriander and simmer until mutton is cooked. Adjust the seasoning.

Remove the mutton pieces and pass the gravy through a soup strainer into a separate *handi*/pan, return the meat to the strained gravy and bring to a boil. Add garam masala and stir.

TO SERVE

Remove to a bowl, garnish with the remaining coriander and serve with Phulka.

———————— • ————————

GURDE KAPOORE

INGREDIENTS

8 *Kapoore*/Sweetbread of Lamb   10 *Gurde*/Lamb Kidney

THE MARINATION

8g/1½ tsp Ginger paste   3g/1 tsp *Haldee*/Turmeric Powder
15g/2½ tsp Garlic Paste   4 *Motti Elaichi*/Black Cardamoms
480ml/2 cups Milk   4 *Lavang*/Cloves
45ml/3 Tbs Brandy   2 *Daalcheeni*/Cinnamon (1")

THE MASALA

75g/6 Tbs *Desi Ghee*/Clarified Butter   1.5g/1/2 tsp *Motti Elaichi*/
8 flakes Garlic (chop)   Black Cardamom Powder
120g/¼ lb Onions (chop)   0.75g/¼ tsp *Lavang*/Clove Powder

15g/1½" piece Ginger (chop)
4 Green Chillies (seed & chop)
3 Tomatoes (large; chop)
4.5g/1½ tsp *Jeera*/Cumin Powder
4.5g/1½ tsp Black Pepper
    (freshly roasted & coarsely ground)

0.75g/¼ tsp *Daalcheeni*/Cinnamon (1")
10g/3 Tbs *Taaza Dhania*/Coriander (chop)
15ml/1Tbsp Lemon Juice
A generous pinch of *Kasoori Methi*/
    Dried Fenugreek Leaf Powder
Salt

Serves: 4
Preparation Time: 3:15 hours
Cooking Time: 25 minutes

PREPARATION

THE OFALLS: Clean, remove the skin , halve, wash, pat dry, put in a panful of milk, add brandy and reserve overnight in the refrigerator. Put the remaining ingredients in a bowl, drain and add the offals, and marinate for 30 minutes.

COOKING

Spread ghee on a *tawa*/griddle, add garlic, sauté over medium heat with a spatula until light golden, add onions and sauté until onions become translucent and glossy. Add ginger and green chillies, stir for a few seconds, add tomatoes and *bhunno*/stir-fry until they become soft (release their juices). Then add the offals along with the marinade and *bhunno*/stir-fry, until the masala nappes the offals. Sprinkle cumin, pepper, cardamom, clove and cinnamon powders, stir, add salt, and stir. Now add coriander and stir, turning with the spatula to incorporate. Remove and adjust the seasoning.

TO SERVE

Remove to flat dish and serve with Phulka, Chappati or Tandoori Roti.

———————— • ————————

MEAT BELIRAM

INGREDIENTS

1.2 kg/ 2²/₃ lb Spring Lamb (assorted cuts)
600 2 2/3 cups *Dahi*/Yoghurt
500g/3 cups Onions
70g/ 7 Tbs Ginger

5 *Lavang*/Cloves
2 sticks *Daalcheeni*/Cinnamon (1-inch)
Salt
10g/ 2 tsp *Kashmiri Deghi Mirch* (or Paprika)

50g/5 Tbs Garlic
10 *Chotti Elaichi*/Green Cardamom

125g/ ²/₃ cup Ghee
15g/ 7½ tsp Coriander seeds

Serves : 4
Preparation Time : 2 hours
Cooking Time : 1-15 hours

PREPARATION

THE LAMB : Clean and cut breast and saddle into 1½-inch chunks; clean chops.

THE YOGHURT : Whisk in a large bowl.

THE VEGETABLES : Peel, wash and slice onions. Scrape, wash and finely chop ginger. Peel and chop garlic.

THE MARINATION : Mix all the ingredients, except coriander seeds and ghee, with yoghurt and leave the lamb chunks in this marinade for 1:45 hours.

COOKING

Heat *ghee* in a *handi*, add coriander seeds and sauté over medium heat until they begin to crackle. Transfer the lamb, along with the marinade, bring to a boil, stirring constantly, then cover and simmer, stirring at regular intervals, until the meat is tender. Uncover, increase to medium heat and *bhunno* until the fat leaves the masala. Adjust the seasoning.

TO SERVE

Remove to a dish and serve with Tandoori Roti.

———————— • ————————

THIPPARANWALA MEAT

INGREDIENTS

750g/1 lb 11oz Shoulder of Kid/Lamb
   (boned 1½ chunks)
250g/9 oz *Shalgam*/Turnips (1½ chunks)
75g/2½ oz *Desi Ghee*/Clarified Butter
8 *Chotti Elaichi*/Green Cardamom

30g/5 tsp Garlic Paste (strain)
15g/2½ tsp Ginger Paste (strain)
Salt
12g/4 tsp *Dhania*/Coriander Powder
3g/1 tsp Red Chilli Powder

5 *Lavang*/Cloves
2 *Mott Elaichi*/Black Cardamom
2 sticks *Daalcheeni*/Cinnamon (1")
2 *Tej Patta*/Bay leaves
300g/11 oz Onions (thin slices)

3g/1 tsp *Haldee*/Turmeric Powder
600ml/2½ cups Fresh Tomato Pureé
1 litre/4¼ cups Clear Mutton Stock (or water)
1.5g/½ tsp *Chotti Elaichi*/Green
    Cardamom powder

The Garnish

10g/1" piece Ginger (juliennes)
3.25g/1 Tb *Taaza Dhania*/Coriander (leaves)
1.5g/½ tsp Black Pepper (freshly roasted & coarsely ground)

Serves: 4
Preparation Time: 35 minutes
Cooking Time: 1:30 hours

COOKING

Heat *ghee* in a *handi*/pan, add green cardamom, cloves, black cardamom, cinnamon, bay leaves, stir over medium heat until the green cardamom changes colour, add two-thirds of the onions, sauté until golden brown, add the meat, increase to high heat and *bhunno*/stir-fry to sear for 2-3 minutes. Reduce to medium heat, add the ginger and garlic pastes, stir for 30 seconds, add the remaining onions and salt, stir, reduce to low heat, cover and cook, stirring occasionally, for 20 minutes. Uncover, increase to medium heat, add turnips, *bhunno*/stir-fry until the liquid evaporates, add coriander, red chilli and turmeric powders (dissolved in 60ml/¼ cup of water) and *bhunno*/stir-fry until the liquid evaporates. Now add tomato pureé, *bhunno*/stir-fry until the fat leaves the sides again, add stock (or water), bring to a boil, reduce to low heat, cover and simmer, stirring occasionally, until the meat and turnips are cooked. Remove, adjust the seasoning, sprinkle cardamom and stir.

TO SERVE

Remove to a bowl, garnish with coriander and ginger, sprinkle pepper and serve with Phulka or Tandoori Roti.

MAAH CHHOLE di DAAL

INGREDIENTS

200g/1 cup *Urad Daal* (whole)
30g/1 oz *Rajmah*/Red Kidney Beans
30g/1 oz *Channa Daal*
Salt
30g/5 tsp Ginger Paste (strain)

30g/5 tsp Garlic Paste (strain)
400g/14 oz Tomato Purée
3g/1 tsp Red Chilli Powder
180g/¾ cup Butter (unsalted)
120ml/½ cup Cream

Serves: 4
Preparation Time: 2:30 hours
Cooking Time: at least 5-6 hours (preferably overnight)

PREPARATION

THE LENTILS: Pick, wash repeatedly, to remove polish, in running water until you get a clear fluid. Drain, replenish with fresh water and reserve for an hour. Then bring to boil, and continue to boil for a couple of minutes. Remove and reserve in the same water for an hour. Drain and keep aside.

COOKING

Put the drained lentils in a *handi*/pan, add 3 litres/12½ cups of water, bring to boil, reduce to very, very low heat, cover and simmer until cooked (approx 3½-4 hours). Ideally, it should be left on a charcoal *angeethi* or on top of a *tandoor* after the day cooking is over. Uncover, remove the scum, increase to low heat, and begin the final phase of cooking by mashing the lentils against the sides with a wooden spoon (approx 45 minutes). As you do that, scrape off the lentils that cling to the sides as the liquid diminishes and incorporate into the simmering daal. Now add 120g/½ cup of butter, ginger and garlic pastes, tomato purée, red chillies and salt, and simmer, stirring at regular intervals, for 1-1½ hours. Stir-in cream, remove and adjust the seasoning.

TO SERVE

Remove to a bowl, garnish with the remaining butter and serve with Tandoori Roti or Phulka.

Maah Chhole di Daal (*Lentil*)

Shikampur Pulao (*Rice delicacy*)

Qorma Pulao (*Rice delicacy*)

Tarkhewala Dahi (*Yoghurt*)

Dahi Wada (*Yoghurt*)

Sutpurrah (*Snack*)

Samosa (*Snack*)

Gaajar ka Halwa (*Dessert*)

CHHOLLIAN di DAAL LAUKI NAAL

INGREDIENTS

250g/1¼ cups *Channa Daal*
20g/2Tbsp Garlic (chopped)
15g/1½Tbsp Ginger (chopped)
3g/1tsp *Haldee*/ Turmeric Powder
4 Green Chillies (seeded and chopped)
Salt
400g/14 oz *Lauki*/Bottle Gourd
4 *Motti Elaichi*/Black Cardamom
2 *Tej Patta*/Bay Leaves

65g/5 Tbs *Desi Ghee* (Clarified Butter)
4 Whole Red Chillies
3g/1½ tsp *Jeera*/Cumin Seeds
3g/1tsp Red Chilli Powder
100g/ 2/3 cups Onions
10g/3 Tbs *Taaza Dhania*/Coriander (chop)
15ml/1Tbsp Lemon Juice
5g/1Tbs *Pudina*/ Mint Leaves (chopped)

Serves: 4
Preparation Time: 55 minutes
Cooking Time: 45 minutes

PREPARATION

THE VEGETABLES: Peel, seed and cut the *lauki* into diamond shape. Peel and slice the onions.
THE LENTIL: Pick, wash in running water and soak for half an hour. Drain.

COOKING

Put the drained channa daal in a *handi*, add salt, turmeric powder and water (approx 2 litres/8⅓ cups). Bring to a boil, reduce heat and remove the scum. Add two-thirds of ginger, garlic and half of the green chillies. Cover and simmer until the daals are cooked and two-thirds of the liquid has evaporated. Mash the lentils lightly against the sides with a wooden spoon. Add the sliced onions, bay leaves and cardamom. Add the lauki. Remove when the lauki is cooked and adjust the seasoning.

THE TEMPERING

Heat ghee in a *handi*/pan add the jeera and sauté over medium heat until they begin to crackle. Add the whole red chillies. Add the remaining ginger and sauté, then add the rest of the green chillies and *bhunno*/stir-fry over medium heat briefly. Transfer the cooked lentils, add lemon juice and adjust the seasoning.

TO SERVE

Remove to four individual bowls, garnish with mint and coriander and serve as an accompaniment.

———————— • ————————

TARKHEWALI DAAL

INGREDIENTS

200g/1 cup *Urad Daal Dhulee*/
   Husked (soak for 30 minutes)
200g/1 cup *Arhar Daal* (soak for 30 minutes)

3g/1 tsp Red Chilli Powder
1.5g/½ tsp *Haldee*/Turmeric Powder
Salt

The Tempering

50g/¼ cup *Desi Ghee*/Clarified Butter
2g/1 tsp *Jeera*/Cumin Seeds
4 flakes Garlic (chop)
120g/¼ lb Onions (chop)
10g/1" piece Ginger (chop)

4 Green Chillies (seed & chop)
150g/5 oz Tomatoes (chop)
3.25g/1 Tbs *Taaza Dhania*/
   Coriander (finely chop)

Serves: 4
Preparation Time: 45 minutes
Cooking Time: 45 minutes

COOKING

Drain and put the lentils in a *handi*/pan, add 1.25 litres/5¼ cups and the remaining ingredients, bring to a boil, reduce to low heat and remove the scum. Then cover and simmer, stirring occasionally until the lentils are cooked, but not mashed.

To prepare the tempering, heat ghee in a frying pan, add cumin, stir over medium heat until it begins to pop, add garlic and *bhunno*/stir-fry until light golden. Now add onions, *bhunno*/stir-fry until onions are translucent and glossy, add ginger and green chillies, and *bhunno*/stir-fry until onions are light golden. Then add tomatoes, *bhunno*/stir-fry until the moisture evaporates, add coriander and stir. Pour the tempering on the cooked daal, stir to incorporate, remove and adjust the seasoning

TO SERVE

Garnish with chopped coriander leaves, *rogan*/chilli oil and serve hot with hot Phulkas.

—————— • ——————

PINDI CHANNA

INGREDIENTS

400g/14 oz *Kabuli Channa*/Chickpeas
A generous pinch Soda Bi-carb
75ml/5 Tbs Cooking Oil
2.5g/1 tsp *Ajwain*/Carom Seeds
20g/1 Tbs *Besan*/Gramflour
15g/5 tsp *Anaardaana*/
    Pomegranate Powder
6g/2 tsp *Amchoor*/Mango Powder

3g/1 tsp Red Chilli Powder
3g/1 tsp *Kaala Namak*/
    Black Rock Salt Powder
3g/2 tsp *Kasoori Methi*/
    Dried Fenugreek Leaf Powder
3g/1 tsp *Jeera*/Cumin Powder
Salt

The Potli

6 *Motti Elaichi*/Black Cardamom
4 sticks *Daalcheeni*/Cinnamon Powder
4 *Lavang*/Cloves

20g/2" piece Ginger (crush)
5g/2 tsp Tea Leaves

The Garnish

2 Tomatoes (medium; cut into wedges)
1 Onion (medium; cut into roundels
    & separate rings)
2 Green Chillies (slit & seed)

3 Lemons (cut into wedges)
10g/1" piece Ginger (juliennes; soak in
    30ml/2 Tbs lemon juice)

Serves: 4
Preparation Time: 2:30 hours
Cooking Time: 1:15 Hours

PREPARATION

THE CHANNA: Put in a *handi*/pan, cover with water and reserve for an hour. Then bring to a boil, continue to boil for 2 minutes, remove and reserve in the same water for an hour*. Drain just prior to cooking.

THE POTLI: Put all the ingredients in a small piece of muslin and secure with string to make a pouch.

COOKING

Add 1 litre/4¼ cups of fresh water to the drained channa, bring to a boil, reduce to low heat, and remove the scum. Then add 20 ml/4 tsp of oil and the potli, cover and simmer until cooked but firm (make sure the channa does not get mashed, nor the skin begins to peel). Remove and keep aside.

To prepare the tempering, heat the remaining oil in a *kadhai*/wok, add ajwain, stir over medium heat until it begins to crackle, add gramflour and *bhunno*/stir-fry until it emits its unique aroma. Then add the remaining ingredients, stir for a minute, add the cooked channa and stir until well mixed. Remove and adjust the seasoning.

TO SERVE

Remove to a serving dish, garnish with tomatoes, onion rings, green chillies, lemon and ginger, and serve with Bhatoora or Kulcha.

* Note: This method is recommended above the traditional soaking overnight. It helps reduce flatulence-causing solubles in lentils.

—————— • ——————

LOBIA

INGREDIENTS

250g/1¼ cup *Lobia*/ White Kidney Beans
3g/1tsp *Haldee*/Turmeric Powder
3g/1½ tsp *Jeera*/ Cumin Seeds
90g/7 Tbs *Desi Ghee* (Clarified Butter)
4 Whole Red Chillies
20g/3¼ tsp Garlic (chopped)
15g/2½ tsp Ginger (chopped)
3g/1 tsp *Kuta Dhania*/Coriander
    Seeds Crushed

3g/1 tsp Red Chilli Powder
Salt
200g/7 oz Tomato (chopped)
3g/1 tsp Black Cardamom Powder
1.5g/½ tsp Black Pepper Powder
50g/¼ cup Butter (unsalted)
60ml/¼ cup Cream
15ml/3 tsp Lemon Juice

The Potli

6 *Motti Elaichi*/Black Cardamoms
4 sticks *Daalcheeni*/Cinnamon Powder

4 *Lavang*/Cloves
4 Green Chilli (seeded and chopped fine)

The Garnish

2 Tomatoes (medium; cut into juliennes)
2 Green Chillies (slit & seed)
3 Lemons (cut into wedges)

10g/1" piece Ginger (juliennes; soak in
   30ml/2 Tbs lemon juice)

Serves: 4
Preparation Time: 1:30 hours
Cooking Time: 1:15 Hours

PREPARATION

THE LOBIA (WHITE KIDNEY BEANS): Pick, wash in running water. Put in a *handi*/pan, and reserve for an hour. Drain.

THE POTLI: Put all the ingredients in a small piece of muslin and secure with string to make a pouch.

COOKING

Add 1 litre/4¼ cups of fresh water to the drained lobia, bring to a boil, reduce to low heat, and remove the scum. Then add the potli, cover and simmer cooking by mashing the lentils against the sides with a wooden spoon. Remove and keep aside.

Heat ghee (clarified butter) in a *handi*/pan, add whole red chillies and cumin seeds, stir over medium heat until the seeds begin crackle, add the garlic and ginger pastes, sauté until golden brown, add coriander powder, red chilli powder and salt (all dissolved in 60ml/¼ cup of water), stir for 30 seconds, add chopped tomato and *bhunno*/stir-fry until the fat leaves the sides. Now add lobia (white kidney beans), bring to a boil, reduce to low heat and cook for 6 to 7 minutes. Add the butter, sprinkle black cardamom and black pepper powders, crushed cumin seeds and stir. Stir-in cream, remove and adjust the seasoning.

TO SERVE

Remove to a serving dish, garnish with tomato juliennes, green chillies, lemon and ginger, and serve with Bhatoora or Kulcha.

RAJMAH

INGREDIENTS

250g/1¼ cups Rajmah (Red Kidney Beans)
4 *Motti Elaichi*/Black Cardamom
2 *Tej Patta*/Bay Leaves
90g/7 Tbs *Desi Ghee* (Clarified Butter)
4 Whole Red Chillies
3g/1½ tsp *Jeera*/Cumin Seeds
180g/1⅔ cups Onions
30g/5 tsp Garlic Paste (strained)

30g/5 tsp Ginger Paste (strained)
3g/1 tsp Coriander Powder
3g/1 tsp Red Chilli Powder
Salt
200g/7 oz Fresh Tomato Purée
3g/1 tsp Black Cardamom Powder
1.5g/ 1/2 tsp Black Pepper Powder

The Garnish

10g/1" piece Ginger

6.5g/2 Tbs Coriander

Serves: 4
Preparation Time: 2 hours
Cooking Time: 45 minutes

PREPARATION

THE RAJMAH (RED KIDNEY BEANS): Pick, wash in running water, drain and soak overnight. Drain, add 1½ litres/6½ cups of water and bring to a boil. Remove scum, reduce to low heat, add whole black cardamom and bay leaves, boil until cooked. Remove black cardamom and bay leaves.

THE GRAVY: Wipe the whole red chillies with a moist cloth. Peel, wash and finely chop onions.

THE GARNISH: Scrape, wash and cut ginger into fine juliennes. Clean, wash and finely chop coriander.

COOKING

Heat ghee (clarified butter) in a *handi*/pan, add whole red chillies and cumin seeds, stir over medium heat until the seeds begin crackle, add onions and sauté until light golden. Then add the garlic and ginger pastes, sauté until onions are golden brown, add coriander powder, red chilli powder and salt (all dissolved in 60ml/¼ cup of water), stir for 30 seconds, add tomato purée and *bhunno*/stir-fry until the fat leaves the sides. Now add the rajmah, bring to a boil, reduce to low heat and cook for 6 to 7 minutes. Sprinkle black cardamom and black pepper powders and stir. Remove and adjust the seasoning.

TO SERVE

Transfer the Rajmah to a service bowl, garnish with ginger and coriander and serve as an accompaniment.

MURG SHIKAMPUR PULAO

INGREDIENTS

8 Breasts of Chicken (60g/2 oz each)
45g/1½ oz Yoghurt
15g/2½ tsp Garlic Paste (strain)
10g/1¾ tsp Ginger Paste (strain)
5g/1 tsp Green Chilli Paste

Salt
25g/2 Tbs *Desi Ghee*/Clarified Butter
Desi Ghee/Clarified Butter to grease
   roasting tray

The Filling

45g/1½ oz *Paneer* (grate)
30g/1 oz Britannia Cheese (grate)
30g/1 oz Pistachio (blanch, cool,
   peel & cut into slivers)
30g/1 oz Almonds Flakes
5ml/1 tsp Honey
4 Green Chillies (seed & finely chop)

3.25g/1 Tbs *Taaza Dhania*/
   Coriander (chop)
0.5g/1 tsp *Zaafraan*/Saffron
(sun-dry & powder)
0.75g/¼tsp *Chotti Elaichi*/
   Green Cardamom Powder

The Rice

400g/2 cups Basmati Rice (soak in
   water for 30 minutes)
Salt
15ml/1 Tbs Lemon Juice
5g/½" piece Ginger (juliennes)
4 Green Chillies (seed & cut into thin strips)
0.5g/1 tsp *Zaafraan*/Saffron
30ml/2 Tbs Milk
Slivers of Roasted Pistachio for garnish
Toasted Almond Flakes for garnish

The Bouquet Garni

8 *Chotti Elaichi*/Green Cardamom
5 *Lavang*/Cloves
3 *Motti Elaichi*/Black Cardamom

2 sticks *Daalcheeni*/Cinnamon (1")
4 *Tej Patta*/Bay Leaf

The Jhol/Cooking Liquor

120ml/½ cup Clear Chicken Stock
50g/¼ cup *Desi Ghee*/Clarified Butter
30ml/2 Tbs Cream
2.25g/¾ tsp *Chotti Elaichi*/
   Green Cardamom Powder
1.5g/½ tsp *Daalcheeni*/Cinnamon Powder

0.75g/¼ tsp *Javitri*/Mace Powder
1 drop *Kewra*
45ml/3 Tbs Lemon Juice
Salt

Serves: 4
Preparation Time: 1:30 hours
Cooking Time: 25-30 minutes

PREPARATION

THE CHICKEN: Clean, remove the skin, bone, wash and pat dry. With a sharp knife slice each breast horizontally to obtain two supremes. Then flatten with a bat.

THE CHICKEN MARINATION: Put all the ingredients in a bowl, mix well, evenly rub the breasts with the marinade and reserve for 15 minutes.

THE FILLING: Mix all the ingredients and divide into 16 equal portions.

THE STUFFING: Place a portion of the filling at a narrow end of each breast and roll tightly to make paupiettes.

THE CHICKEN: Grease a roasting tray, arrange the stuffed chicken breasts, cover the tray with foil and roast in a pre-heated oven (300°F) for 8-10 minutes. Remove the breasts. Strain the jus and reserve for the jhol.

THE JHOL/COOKING LIQUOR: Put stock in a *handi*/pan, add the jus and ghee, and bring to a boil. Add the remaining ingredients and bring to just under a boil. Remove and keep aside.

THE SAFFRON: Crush the threads with a pestle or the back of a spoon, soak in lukewarm milk and then make a paste.

THE BOUQUET GARNI: Put all the ingredients in a mortar and pound with a pestle to break the spices, fold in a piece of muslin and secure with enough string for it to hang over the rim of the handi/pan.

THE OVEN: Pre-heat to 350°F.

COOKING

To prepare the rice, boil 1.5 litres/6¼ cups of water in a *handi*/pan, add the bouquet garni and salt, stir, add rice, bring to a boil, reduce to medium heat, add lemon juice and continue to boil, stirring occasionally, until nine-tenths cooked. Drain, and keep aside.

ASSEMBLING

Put one-third of the rice in a *handi*/pan, arrange half the chicken paupiettes on top, spread half the jhol, ginger juliennes, green chillies and saffron on the chicken. Spread another one-third of the rice, arrange the remaining chicken paupiettes, spread the remaining jhol, ginger juliennes, green chillies and saffron on top. Spread the remaining rice, place a moist cloth on top, cover with lid and seal with atta dough. Now cook until steam starts seeping out of the dough. Remove and keep aside.

FINISHING

Put the sealed *handi*/pan on *dum* in the pre-heated oven for 15-20 minutes.

TO SERVE

Break the seal, remove the lid, garnish with roasted pistachio and toasted almonds and serve from the *handi*/pan itself.

———————— • ————————

NARANGI PULAO

INGREDIENTS

400g/2 cups Basmati Rice
  (soak in water for 30 minutes)
15ml/1 Tbs Lemon Juice
5g/½" piece Ginger (juliennes)

4 Green Chillies (seed & cut into
  thin strips)
6.5g/2 Tbs *Taaza Dhania*/Coriander (chop)
Salt

The Bouquet Garni

6 *Chotti Elaichi*/Green Cardamom
4 *Motti Elaichi*/Black Cardamom
3 *Lavang*/Cloves

2 sticks *Daalcheeni*/Cinnamon (1")
3 *Tej Patta*/Bay Leaf

The Chicken

8 Legs of Chicken (bone & obtain
  2 tikka from each thigh & drumstick)
65g/5 Tbs *Desi Ghee*/Clarified Butter
20g/3½ tsp Garlic Paste (strain)
15g/2½ tsp Ginger Paste (strain)
125g/½ cup *Dahi*/Yoghurt
3g/1 tsp Red Chilli Powder
Salt
120ml/½ cup Orange Juice
  (fresh; unsweetened)

60ml/¼ cup Cream
2.25g/¾ tsp *Chotti Elaichi*/
  Green Cardamom Powder
1.5g/½ tsp *Daalcheeni*/Cinnamon Powder
0.75g/¼ tsp *Javitri*/Mace Powder
1g/2 tsp *Zaafraan*/Saffron
30ml/2 Tbs Milk
1 drop *Kewra*

The Orange Peel

Peel off one orange (remove the white
  membrane from the rind & cut into juliennes)

45ml/1½ oz *Dahi*/Yoghurt (whisk)

Serves: 4
Preparation Time: 1:30 hours
Cooking Time: 25-30 minutes

PREPARATION

THE SAFFRON: Crush the threads with a pestle or the back of a spoon, soak in lukewarm milk and then make a paste.

THE BOUQUET GARNI: Put both the ingredients in a mortar and pound with a pestle to break the spices, fold in a piece of muslin and secure with enough string for it to hang over the rim of the *handi*/pan.

THE YOGHURT MIXTURE: Put yoghurt in a bowl, add red chillies and salt, whisk to mix well.

THE ORANGE PEEL: Reserve in yoghurt for 1 hour.

THE CHICKEN: Heat ghee in a *handi*/pan, add orange peel, sauté over medium heat for 30 seconds, remove and keep aside. In the same ghee, add garlic and ginger, stir until the moisture evaporates, add chicken, increase to high heat and sear for a minute. Remove *handi*/pan from heat, stir-in the yoghurt mixture, return *handi*/pan to heat and *bhunno*/stir-fry until specks of fat begin to appear on the surface. Then add 360ml/1½ cups of water, bring to a boil, reduce to low heat and simmer until the chicken is half cooked. Stir-in orange juice and simmer until the chicken is three-fourths ths cooked. Remove *handi*/pan from heat, stir-in the remaining ingredients, mix well and adjust the seasoning.

COOKING

To prepare the rice, boil 1.5 litres/6¼ cups of water in a *handi*/pan, add the bouquet garni and salt, stir, add rice, bring to a boil, reduce to medium heat, add lemon juice and continue to boil, stirring occasionally, until nine-tenths cooked. Drain, and keep aside.

ASSEMBLING

Put one-third of the rice in a *handi*/pan, spread half of the chicken and liquor on top, and sprinkle half the ginger juliennes, green chillies and coriander on the chicken. Spread another one-third of the rice, spread the remaining chicken and liquor on top, and sprinkle the remaining ginger juliennes, green chillies and coriander on the chicken. Spread the remaining rice and evenly spread the orange peel on top. Place a moist cloth on top, cover with lid and seal with atta dough. Now cook until steam starts seeping out of the dough. Remove and keep aside.

FINISHING

Put the sealed *handi*/pan on *dum* in the pre-heated oven for 15-20 minutes.

TO SERVE

Break the seal and serve from the *handi*/pan itself.

QORMA PULAO

INGREDIENTS

The Khorma

16 *Chaamp*/Kid/Lamb Chops (2-rib)
90g/6 Tbs *Desi Ghee*/Clarified Butter
8 *Chotti Elaichi*/Green Cardamoms
4 *Motti Elaichi*/Black Cardamoms
6 *Lavang*/Cloves
2 sticks *Daalcheeni*/Cinnamon (1")
2 *Tej Patta*/Bay Leaf

6g/2 tsp Red Chilli Powder
150g/5 oz *Dahi*/Yoghurt (whisk)
Salt
1 litre/4¼ cups Clear Kid/
  Lamb Stock (very thin)
3.25g/1 Tbs *Taaza Dhania*/
  Coriander (chop)

2g/1 tsp *Jeera*/Cumin Seeds
200g/7 oz Onions (slice)
30g/5¼ tsp Ginger Paste (strain)
20g/3½ tsp Garlic Paste (strain)

2.5g/1 Tbs *Taaza Pudhina*/Mint (chop)
4 Green Chillies (seed & cut into
 ¹/₈ " thick strips)

The Rice

400g/2 cups Basmati Rice (soak in
 water for 30 minutes)
Salt
15ml/1 Tbs Lemon Juice
5g/½" piece Ginger (juliennes)

4 Green Chillies (seed & cut into thin strips)
1g/2 tsp *Zaafraan*/Saffron
30ml/2 Tbs Milk
Slivers of Roasted Pistachio for garnish
Toasted Almond Flakes for garnish

The Bouquet Garni

8 *Chotti Elaichi*/Green Cardamoms
5 *Lavang*/Cloves
3 *Motti Elaichi*/Black Cardamom

2 sticks *Daalcheeni*/Cinnamon (1")
5 *Tej Patta*/Bay Leaf

Serves: 4
Preparation Time: 1:30 hours (plus time taken to make stock)
Cooking Time: 25-30 hours

PREPARATION

THE QORMA: Heat ghee in a *handi*/pan, add green cardamom, black cardamom, cloves, cinnamon, bay leaf and cumin, and stir over medium heat until the cardamom begins to change colour. Add onions, sauté until translucent and glossy, add the ginger and garlic pastes, sauté until onions are light golden, add red chillies (dissolved in 45ml/3 Tbs of water, *bhunno*/stir-fry until the moisture evaporates, add yoghurt and *bhunno*/stir-fry until specks of fat begin to appear on the surface. Then add meat and salt, increase to high heat and sear for 2-3 minutes. Reduce to low heat, cover and simmer, stirring occasionally, for 15-20 minutes (add small quantities of water, if necessary, to prevent sticking). Uncover, increase to medium heat and *bhunno*/stir-fry until the moisture evaporates. Now add stock, bring to a boil, reduce to low heat and simmer until the meat is cooked (the gravy should be very thin). Add coriander, mint and green chillies, stir for a few seconds. Remove and adjust the seasoning.

THE SAFFRON: Crush the threads with a pestle or the back of a spoon, reserve in 30ml/2 Tbs of water for 15 minutes and then make a paste.

THE BOUQUET GARNI: Put all the ingredients in a mortar and pound with a pestle to break the spices, fold in a piece of muslin and secure with enough string for it to hang over the rim of the *handi*/pan.

THE OVEN: Pre-heat to 350°F.

COOKING

To prepare the rice, boil 1.5 litres/6¼ cups of water in a *handi*/pan, add the bouquet garni and salt, stir, add rice, bring to a boil, reduce to medium heat, add lemon juice and continue to boil, stirring occasionally, until nine-tenths cooked. Drain, and keep aside.

ASSEMBLING

Put one-third of the rice in a *handi*/pan, arrange half of the meat and gravy on top, and sprinkle half the ginger juliennes, green chillies and saffron on the meat. Spread another one-third of the rice, arrange the remaining meat and gravy on top, and sprinkle the remaining ginger juliennes, green chillies and saffron. Spread the remaining rice, place a moist cloth on top, cover with lid and seal with atta dough. Now cook until steam starts seeping out of the dough. Remove and keep aside.

FINISHING

Put the sealed *handi*/pan on *dum* in the pre-heated oven for 15-20 minutes.

TO SERVE

Break the seal, remove the lid, garnish with roasted pistachio and toasted almonds and serve from the *handi*/pan itself.

———— • ————

MOONGPHALI KOFTA PULAO

INGREDIENTS

The Kofta

120g/4 oz *Zimikand*/Yam
30g/1 oz Flour of Roasted Channa
3g/1 tsp Black Pepper (freshly broiled & ground)

Salt
15g/½ oz Butter
Groundnut Oil to deep fry

The Filling

45g/1½ oz Roasted Peanuts (chop)
30g/1 oz Paneer (grate)
3.25g/1 Tbs *Taaza Dhania*/Coriander (chop)

2.5g/1 Tbs *Taaza Pudhina*/Mint (chop)
4 Green Chillies (seed & finely chop)
Salt

The Rice

400g/2 cups Basmati Rice
   (soak in water for 30 minutes)
Salt
15ml/1 Tbs Lemon Juice
5g/½" piece Ginger (juliennes)

4 Green Chillies (seed & cut into thin strips)
6.5g/2 Tbs *Taaza Dhania*/Coriander (chop)
5g/2 Tbs *Taaza Pudhina*/Mint (chop)
15g/½ oz Fried Onions (golden brown)
60g/2 oz Roasted Peanuts

The Bouquet Garni

8 *Chotti Elaichi*/Green Cardamom
4 *Motti Elaichi*/Black Cardamom
3 *Lavang*/Cloves

2 *Daalcheeni*/Cinnamon (1")
1 *Tej Patta*/Bay Leaf

The Jhol/Cooking Liquor

25g/2 Tbs *Desi Ghee*/Clarified Butter
60g/2 oz Onions (chop)
15g/2½ tsp Garlic Paste (strain)
10g/1¾ tsp Ginger Paste (strain)
3g/1 tsp Red Chilli Powder
100g/3 oz Tomatoes (chop)

Salt
60g/2 oz Peanut Butter
45ml/3 Tbs Lemon Juice
1.5g/½ tsp *Chotti Elaichi*/
   Green Cardamom Powder
1 drop *Kewra*

Serves: 4
Preparation Time: 1:30 hours
Cooking Time: 25-30 minutes

PREPARATION

THE YAM: Peel yam, wash, cut into cubes, put in a *handi*/pan, add enough water and boil until cooked (approx 20 minutes). Drain, cool, put in food processor/blender and grind into a smooth paste. Melt butter in a *kadhai*/wok, add the paste and *bhunno*/stir-fry until the moisture has completely evaporated and the yam becomes like a khoya ball. Remove and spread on a flat surface to cool immediately. Then transfer to a bowl, add the remaining ingredients, except cooking oil, mix well, divide into 24 equal portions and make balls.

THE FILLING: Mix all the ingredients in a bowl and divide into 24 equal portions.

THE STUFFING: Flatten each ball between the palms, place a portion of the filling in the middle, and make balls again.

THE FRYING: Heat oil in a *kadhai*/wok and deep fry the kofta over medium heat until golden. Remove to absorbent paper to drain the excess fat.

THE BOUQUET GARNI: Put all the ingredients in a mortar and pound with a pestle to break the spices, fold in a piece of muslin and secure with enough string for it to hang over the rim of the *handi*/pan.

THE JHOL/COOKING LIQUOR: Heat ghee in a *kadhai*/wok, add onions, sauté over medium heat until translucent and glossy, add garlic and ginger, and sauté until the moisture evaporates. Then add red chillies (dissolved in 15ml/1 Tbs of water), *bhunno*/stir-fry until the moisture evaporates, add tomatoes and salt, and *bhunno*/stir-fry until the fat leaves the sides and the tomatoes are mashed. Now add peanut butter and 120ml/½ cup of water, bring to a boil, remove, add lemon juice, cardamom powder and kewra, stir and adjust the seasoning.

THE OVEN: Pre-heat to 350°F.

COOKING

To prepare the rice, boil 1.5 litres/6¼ cups of water in a *handi*/pan, add green cardamom and salt, stir, add rice, bring to a boil, reduce to medium heat, add lemon juice and continue to boil, stirring occasionally, until nine-tenths cooked. Drain, and keep aside.

ASSEMBLING

Put one-third of the rice in a *handi*/pan, arrange half of the kofta and jhol on top, and sprinkle half the ginger juliennes, green chillies, coriander and mint on the chicken. Spread another one-third of the rice, arrange the remaining kofta and jhol on top, and sprinkle the remaining ginger juliennes, green chillies, coriander and mint. Spread the remaining rice, place a moist cloth on top, cover with lid and seal with atta dough. Now cook until steam starts seeping out of the dough. Remove and keep aside.

FINISHING

Put the sealed *handi*/pan on *dum* in the pre-heated oven and cook for 15-20 minutes.

TO SERVE

Break the seal, remove the lid, garnish with fried onions and roasted peanuts and serve from the *handi*/pan itself.

————————————— • —————————————

KABULI CHANNE da PULAO

INGREDIENTS

400g/2 cups Basmati Rice
  (soak in water for 30 minutes)
6 *Chotti Elaichi*/Green Cardamom
15ml/1 Tbs Lemon Juice
5g/½" piece Ginger (juliennes)
4 Green Chillies (seed & cut into thin strips)
6.5g/2 Tbs *Taaza Dhania*/Coriander (chop)
5g/2 Tbs *Taaza Pudhina*/Mint (chop)
Salt
15g/½ oz Fried Onions (golden brown)
200g/7 oz *Kabuli Channa*/Chick Peas

65g/5 Tbs *Desi Ghee*/Clarified Butter
60g/2 oz Onions (chop)
15g/2½ tsp Garlic Paste (strain)
10g/1¾ tsp Ginger Paste (strain)
3g/1 tsp Red Chilli Powder
100g/3 oz Tomatoes (chop)
Salt
15ml/1 Tbs Lemon Juice
1.5g/½ tsp *Chotti Elaichi*/
  Green Cardamom Powder
1 drop *Kewra*

The Bouquet Garni

4 *Motti Elaichi*/Black Cardamom
3 *Lavang*/Cloves

2 sticks *Daalcheeni*/Cinnamon (1")
2 *Tej Patta*/Bay Leaf

Serves: 4
Preparation Time: 30 minutes (plus time taken to prepare *Kabuli Channa*)
Cooking Time: 25-30 minutes

PREPARATION

THE BOUQUET GARNI: Put both the ingredients in a mortar and pound with a pestle to break the spices, fold in a piece of muslin and secure with enough string for it to hang over the rim of the *handi*/pan.

THE KABULI CHANNA/CHICK PEAS: Soak overnight in a *handi*/panful of water. The following morning, drain, cover with fresh water, bring to a boil, continue to boil for 2 minutes, remove and reserve in the same water for an hour. Drain just prior to cooking, put in a *handi*/pan, add the bouquet garni and water (approx 1 litre/3 cups), and boil until cooked.

Heat ghee in a *kadhai*/wok, add onions, sauté over medium heat until translucent and glossy, add garlic and ginger, and sauté until the moisture evaporates. Then add red chillies (dissolved in 15ml/1 Tbs of water), *bhunno*/stir-fry until the moisture evaporates, add tomatoes and salt, and *bhunno*/stir-fry until the fat leaves the sides and the tomatoes are mashed. Now add the boiled channa along with the liquor, bring to a boil, remove, add lemon juice, cardamom powder and kewra, stir and adjust the seasoning.

THE OVEN: Pre-heat to 350°F.

COOKING

To prepare the rice, boil 1.5 litres/6¼ cups of water in a *handi*/pan, add green cardamom and salt, stir, add rice, bring to a boil, reduce to medium heat, add lemon juice and continue to boil, stirring occasionally, until nine-tenths cooked. Drain, and keep aside.

ASSEMBLING

Put half the channa and liquor in a *handi*/pan, spread half of the boiled rice on top, and sprinkle half the ginger juliennes, green chillies, coriander and mint on the rice. Spread the remaining channa and liquor on the rice, spread the remaining rice on top, and sprinkle the remaining ginger juliennes, green chillies, coriander and mint on the rice. Spread the fried onions evenly, place a moist cloth on top, cover with lid and seal with atta dough. Now cook until steam starts seeping out of the dough. Remove and keep aside.

FINISHING

Put the sealed *handi*/pan on *dum* in the pre-heated oven and cook for 15-20 minutes.

TO SERVE

Break the seal and serve from the *handi*/pan itself.

———— • ————

MUTTAR PULAO

INGREDIENTS

400g/2 cups Basmati Rice
15ml/1 Tbs Lemon Juice
30ml/2 Tbs *Kewrapaani*

A generous pinch *Chotti Elaichi*/
   Green Cardamom Powder
A generous pinch *Javitri*/Mace Powder

The Bouquet Garni

18 Black Peppercorns
6 *Chotti Elaichi*/Green Cardamom
5 *Lavang*/Cloves

3 *Motti Elaichi*/Black Cardamom
2 sticks *Daalcheeni*/Cinnamon (1")
2 *Tej Patta*/Bay Leaves

The Green Peas

250g/9 oz Green Peas (boil until al dente)
75g/6 Tbs *Desi Ghee*/Clarified Butter
150g/5 oz Onions (slice)
20g/3¼ tsp Ginger Paste (strain)
20g/3¼ tsp Garlic Paste (strain)

Salt
6 *Chotti Elaichi*/Green Cardamom
5 *Lavang*/Cloves
0.25g/¼ tsp *Zaafraan*/Saffron
    (reserve in 15ml/1 Tbs of water)

Serves: 4
Preparation Time: 35 minutes
Cooking Time: 20 minutes

PREPARATION

THE BOUQUET GARNI: Put ingredients in mortar and pound with pestle to break spices, fold in piece of muslin and secure with enough string for it to hang over rim of *handi*/pan.

THE RICE: Pick rice, wash in running water, drain, transfer to a separate *handi*/pan, add the bouquet garni and reserve for 30 minutes. Drain at the time of cooking. Reserve the bouquet garni.

COOKING

Put 3 litres/12¾ cups of water in a *handi*/pan, add the reserved bouquet garni, salt, stir, sprinkle lemon juice, stir, bring to a boil, add rice and boil over medium heat until almost cooked. Drain, discard the bouquet garni, transfer to a separate *handi*/pan, sprinkle kewrapaani, cardamom and mace, cover and keep aside for 10 minutes.

Meanwhile, heat ghee in a frying pan, add onions, sauté over medium heat until translucent and glossy, add the ginger and garlic pastes, *bhunno*/stir-fry until onions are light golden. Then add green peas and salt, *bhunno*/stir-fry until the moisture evaporates, add green cardamom and cloves, *bhunno*/stir-fry for a minute. Remove, transfer to the *handi*/pan with the rice, sprinkle saffron, mix gently and adjust the seasoning.

TO SERVE

Remove to a service dish with Raita.

AMRITSARI KULCHA

INGREDIENTS

THE DOUGH

400g/14 oz *Maida*/Refined Flour

Salt

750ml/ 3¼ cup Water

100g/½ cup *Desi Ghee*/ Clarified Butter

THE FILLING

175g/6 oz Potatoes

150g/5 oz Cauliflower

35g/1¼ oz *Paneer*

6g/ 2 tsp Ginger (chopped fine)

2g/1 Tbsp Fresh Coriander (chopped fine)

3g/1Tbsp Green Chillies
   (deseed and chopped)

35g/¼ cup Onion (chopped fine)

3g/1 tsp Black Pepper Powder

3g/1tsp *Anaardaana*/*Dried*
   Pomegranate seed Powder

3g/1tsp *Jeera*/Cumin Seeds

3g/1 tsp *Ajwain*/Carom Seeds

3g/1tsp Coriander Seeds
   (freshly broiled and crushed)

3g/1 tsp *Kasuri Methi*/
   Dried Fenugreek leaves

3g/ 1 tsp Garam Masala

Yield: 8 (approx. 8" in diameter)
Preparation Time: 45 minutes
Cooking Time:
   In Tandoor: 3-4 minutes
   In Oven: 10 minutes

PREPARATION

THE POTATOES: Boil, cool, peel and grate

THE CAULIFLOWER: Clean, wash and grate cauliflower. Scrape wash and chop ginger.

THE PANEER: Grate

THE FILLING: Mix all the ingredients in a bowl. Divide into eight equal portions.

THE MAIDA: Sieve with salt into a *paraat*.

THE DOUGH: Make a bay in the sieved maida, pour water in it and start mixing gradually. When fully mixed knead to make a soft- but smooth- dough, cover with a moist cloth and keep aside for 30 minutes. Add half the desi ghee, knead and punch the dough, cover with a moist cloth and keep aside for another 10 minutes. Divide into eight equal portions, make balls and place on a lightly floured surface.

Cover yet again with a moist cloth and keep aside for 5 minutes. Place the balls on a lightly floured surface and flatten each with a rolling pin into round discs (approx 4" diameter). Place a portion of the filling in the middle, enfold the filling and pinch off the excess dough to seal the edges. Then flatten again with a rolling pin (approx 8-inch diameter)

COOKING

Place the round disc on a *gaddi* (cushioned pad), stick inside a moderately hot tandoor and bake for 3-4 minutes. In the pre-heated oven, place on a greased baking tray and bake for 10 minutes.

TO SERVE

Apply desi ghee on the Kulcha as soon as it is removed from the tandoor or oven and serve immediately.

•

BESAN da POORHA

INGREDIENTS

The Batter

300g/2¾ cups *Besan*/Gramflour
Salt
4g/2 tsp *Jeera*/Cumin Seeds

3g/1 tsp Red Chilli Powder
1.5g/a very generous pinch *Heeng*/Asafoetida
Desi Ghee or Mustard Oil to shallow fry

The Topping

150g/5 oz *Paneer*/Cottage Cheese
80g/¾ cup Onions
75g/½ cup Tomatoes

12.5g/4 Tbs Coriander
2 Green Chillies

Serves: 4
Preparation Time: 25 minutes
Cooking Time: 2 minutes per Chillah

PREPARATION

THE BESAN (GRAMFLOUR): Sift along with salt into a bowl, add cumin seeds and red chillies, mix well.

THE ASAFOETIDA: Dissolve in 45 ml of water.

THE BATTER: Mix the dissolved asafoetida and 540ml of water with the besan mixture and make a batter of pouring consistency. Divide into 16 equal portions and keep aside.

THE PANEER: Grate, mash or make small dices and divide into 16 equal portions.

THE VEGETABLES: Peel onions, wash and make small dices. Remove eyes, wash tomatoes, quarter, deseed and make small dices. Clean, wash and finely chop coriander. Remove stems, wash, slit, deseed and finely chop green chillies. Mix all the ingredients in a bowl and divide into 16 equal portions.

COOKING

Heat just enough desi ghee or mustard oil in a small frying pan, spread a portion of the batter to make a pancake with a 4" diameter and shallow fry over low heat for a few seconds. Then sprinkle a portion each of the paneer and vegetables over the surface of the pancake, sprinkle a little desi ghee or mustard oil along the periphery and cook. Lift the pancake and, if perforations are visible and the Chillah is lightly coloured, flip it over. Sprinkle another small quantity of desi ghee or mustard oil and cook for 45 seconds. Fold and remove to absorbent paper to drain off the excess fat. Repeat the process with the remaining portions.

TO SERVE

Remove to a dish and serve with Coriander (60%)-Mint (40%) Chutney or Saunth and accompaniments of your choice.

———————————— • ————————————

BHATURA

INGREDIENTS

400g/ 14 oz Maida/ Flour	25g/2 Tbsp *Dahi*/Yoghurt
100G/4 oz *Suji*/Semolina	10g/2½ tsp Sugar
1g /¼tsp Soda bi-carb	20g/5tsp *Desi Ghee*/ Clarified Butter

3g/ ½ tsp Baking Powder
Salt

Groundnut Oil to grease surface
and to deep fry

Yield: 15
Preparation Time: 1:20 hrs
Cooking Time: 1 minute for each Bhatura

PREPARATION

THE FLOUR: Sieve with semolina, soda bi-carb, baking powder and salt into a paraat.

THE YOGHURT MIXTURE: Whisk together with sugar.

THE DOUGH: Make a bay in the sieved flour, pour water(approx 240ml/1 cup) and the yoghurt mixture in it,and mix gradually. When mixed, knead to make a dough, cover with a moist cloth and keep aside for 50 minutes. Divide the dough into 15 equal portions, make balls and place on a lightly greased surface. Cover and keep aside.

COOKING

Heat oil in a kadhai to smoking point, reduce to medium heat, flatten each ball between lightly oiled palms to make a round disc(approx 5-inch in diameter) and deep fry until golden brown, turning once to ensure it puffs up.

TO SERVE

Serve as they are removed from the *kadhai*.

———————— • ————————

MAKKE di ROTI

INGREDIENTS

225g/2 cups Maize Flour
60g/7Tbsp *Atta*/Whole Wheat Flour
25g/2½Tbsp *Maida*/ Refined Flour

40g/3Tbsp *Desi Ghee*/ Clarified Butter
Salt
Warm Water for kneading

Yields: 8
Preparation Time: 45 minutes
Cooking Time:
    In Tandoor: 2-3 minutes
    In Oven: 4-5 minutes

PREPARATION

Sieve together maize flour, atta, maida and salt into a *paraat*/ mixing bowl. Add warm water gradually and knead to a smooth dough. Cover with a moist cloth and rest for half an hour.

Divide the dough into eight equal portions, make balls, dust with flour cover and keep aside for five minutes.

THE OVEN: Pre-heat to 375°F

COOKING

Flatten each ball between palms or alternatively roll with a rolling pin to make a round disc (approx 6" diameter but should be thicker than a paratha). Sprinkle flour to prevent sticking. Place the roti on a gaddi (cushioned pad) and stick inside moderately hot tandoor and bake for 2 minutes. In the pre-heated oven, place on a greased baking tray and bake for 5-6 minutes.

TO SERVE

Remove from tandoor, apply melted ghee on each Roti and serve with Sarson da Saag.

KHASTA ROTI

INGREDIENTS

225g/2 cups *Atta*/ Whole Wheat Flour	7.5g/1 Tbsp *Ajwain*/Carom Seeds
110g/1 cup *Maida*/ Refined Flour	40g/3 Tbsp *Desi Ghee*/Clarified Butter
110g/1 cup *Suji*/ Semolina	Salt
105g/½ cup *Desi Ghee*/ Clarified Butter	Sugar
500ml/2 cups Milk	Water

Yields: 10
Preparation Time: 55 minutes
Cooking Time: 10 minutes

PREPARATION

Dissolve salt and sugar in warm milk. Soak the semolina in the milk, add ajwain and leave aside for 10 minutes. Sieve the atta and maida together onto a *paraat*/mixing bowl, add ghee and knead. Add the semolina soaked in milk to the *paraat/* mixing bowl and knead, adding water gradually to a smooth dough. Cover with a moist cloth and rest for half an hour.

Divide the dough into ten equal portions, make balls, dust with flour, cover and keep aside for five minutes.

THE OVEN: Pre-heat to 425°F

COOKING

Roll each ball into a round disc(approx 6"diameter). Perforate the disc with a fork.

Place the roti on a *gaddi* (cushioned pad) and stick inside a moderately hot tandoor and bake for 3-4 minutes. In the pre-heated oven, place on a greased baking tray and bake for 6-7 minutes.

TO SERVE

Remove from tandoor, smear with desi ghee and serve immediately.

———————— • ————————

MISSI ROTI

INGREDIENTS

100g/½ cup Cooked and mashed
  Channa Daal
100g/½ cup Cooked and mashed
  husked *Moong Daal*
30g/3 Tbsp *Atta/* Whole wheat Flour
20g/2 Tbsp *Maida/*Refined Flour
40g/5 Tbsp Onion (chopped fine)
3 Green Chillies (chopped fine)

15g/1 Tbsp Ginger (chopped fine)
15g/4½ Tbsp Fresh Coriander
  (washed and chopped fine)
1.5g/½ tsp *Haldee/*Turmeric Powder
3g/1 tsp Red Chilli Powder
Salt
40g/3 Tbsp *Desi Ghee/* Clarified Butter

Yield : 8
Preparation Time: 50 minutes
Cooking Time: 3-4 minutes

PREPARATION

Put the lentils in a food processor and make into a fine paste. In a mixing bowl sift the atta and maida. Add the daal paste and all the other ingredients except ghee. Mix thoroughly, adding just enough water to knead into a soft pliable dough.

Divide the dough into eight equal portions, make balls, dust with atta, cover with a moist cloth and keep aside for five minutes.

THE OVEN: Pre-heat to 400°F

COOKING

Flatten each ball between palms to a round disc (approx 5" in diameter), place on a *gaddi*(cushioned pad), stick inside a moderately hot tandoor and bake for 3-4 minutes. In the pre-heated oven, place on a greased baking tray and bake for 5-6 minutes.

TO SERVE

Remove from the tandoor, apply ghee on it and serve.

KESAR di PARONTHI NAAN

INGREDIENTS

450g/ 1lb Refined Flour
A pinch of Soda bi-carb
1 Egg
150ml/²⁄₃ cup Milk
10g/2 ½ tsp Sugar
Salt
30ml/2 Tbs Groundnut Oil

100g/7 Tbsp Butter
25g/2 Tbsp *Dahi*/Yoghurt
Flour to dust
Ghee to grease baking tray
    and brush the bread
1g/2 tsp *Zaafraan*/Saffron
15ml/1Tbsp Milk

Yield : 6
Preparation Time: 2 hrs 15 minutes
Cooking Time: 2-3 minutes

PREPARATION

THE FLOUR: Sieve with salt, soda bi-carb and baking powder into a *paraat*/mixing bowl.

THE EGG MIXTURE: Break the egg in a bowl; add sugar, yoghurt and milk; whisk.

THE SAFFRON: Dissolve in 15 ml warm milk.

THE DOUGH: Make a bay in the sieved flour, pour water (approx 200ml/¾ cup +4 tsp) in it and start mixing gradually. When fully mixed, knead to make a dough. Add the egg mixture and incorporate gradually. When fully mixed, knead to make a soft but non-sticky dough. Cover with a moist cloth and rest for 10 minutes. Then add oil, knead and keep aside for 2 hrs to allow the dough to rise.

Divide into 6 equal portions, make balls and place on a lightly floured surface.

Roll out each ball into 9-inch diameter. Grease the disc with melted butter and dust with flour. Hold from two ends and gather ensuring there are many folds and roll it up into a pedha and then flatten slightly. Rest for another 5 minutes.

Flatten each pedha between the palms to make a round disc and then stretch to give the shape of an elongated oval. Brush with saffron.

COOKING

Place the Naan on a *gaddi* (cushioned pad), stick inside a moderately hot tandoor and bake for 3 minutes. In a pre-heated oven, place on a greased baking tray and bake for 10 minutes.

TO SERVE

Apply saffron and melted butter on the Naan as soon as it is removed from the tandoor or oven and serve immediately.

TARKHEWALA DAHI

INGREDIENTS

1.2 litres/5 cups *Dahi*/Yoghurt
45ml/3 Tbs Cooking Oil
2.25g/½ tsp *Rai*/Black Mustard Seeds
1g/½ tsp *Dhania*/Coriander Seeds
8 Red Chillies
16 *Kaari Patta*/Curry Leaf
45g/1½ oz Onions (finely chop)

10g/1" piece Ginger (finely chop)
2 Green Chillies (seed & finely chop)
3g/1 tsp *Haldee*/Turmeric Powder
1.5g/½ tsp Red Chilli Powder
75g/1½ oz Tomatoes (finely chop)
Salt

Serves: 4
Preparation Time: 30 minutes (plus time taken to obtain hung yoghurt)
Cooking Time: 5-6 minutes

PREPARATION

THE YOGHURT: Hang in muslin and once the whey is completely drained, transfer to a bowl, level with a spatula and reserve in the refrigerator until cool.

COOKING

Heat oil in a *kadhai*/wok, add mustard, coriander and red chillies, and stir over medium heat until chillies become bright red. Add curry leaf, stir until they stop spluttering, add onions, sauté until translucent and glossy, add ginger and green chillies, and sauté until onions are lightly coloured. Then add turmeric and red chilli powder (dissolved in 30ml/2 Tbs of water), and stir until the moisture evaporates. Now add tomatoes and salt, and *bhunno*/stir-fry until the moisture evaporates, remove and pour over the yoghurt cheese. Serve as an accompanment.

ANANAS ka RAITA

INGREDIENTS

250g/1 cup *Dahi*/Yoghurt
2 Pineapple Rings (canned)

Salt

PREPARATION

Whisk yoghurt in a bowl. Drain, chop pineapple rings, add to the yoghurt along with salt and mix well. Adjust the seasoning. Serve as an accompaniment.

LAUKI ka RAITA

INGREDIENTS

250g/1 cup *Dahi*/Yoghurt
100g/2 oz Bottle Gourd
2 Green Chillies
1.5g/½ tsp White Pepper Powder

1.5g/½ tsp *Jeera*/Cumin Powder
   (freshly broiled & powdered)
A pinch Black Rock Salt Powder
Salt

PREPARATION

THE VEGETABLES: Peel, wash, quarter, core and boil in salted boiling water until cooked. Drain, refresh in iced water, drain and squeeze in a cloth napkin to remove any residual moisture. Remove stems, wash, slit, deseed and finely chop green chillies.

THE RAITA: Whisk yoghurt in a bowl, add the cooked bottle gourd and the remaining ingredients, mix well. Adjust the seasoning. Serve as an accompaniment.

KACHUMBAR RAITA

INGREDIENTS

250g/1 cup *Dahi*/Yoghurt
1 Onion (small)
1 Tomato (small)
2 Green Chillies
¼ Cucumber (medium)

3.25g/1 Tbs *Taaza Dhania*/Coriander Leaves
1.5g/½ tsp White Pepper Powder
1.5g/½ tsp *Jeera*/Cumin Powder
   (freshly broiled & powdered)
Salt

PREPARATION

THE VEGETABLES: Peel, wash and dice onions. Remove eye, wash, quarter, deseed and dice tomatoes. Peel, wash, quarter, deseed and dice cucumber. Remove stems, wash, slit, deseed and finely chop green chillies. Clean and wash coriander leaves (the stems have to be removed before weighing).

THE RAITA: Whisk yoghurt in a bowl, add the vegetables and the remaining ingredients, mix well. Adjust the seasoning. Serve as an accompaniment.

———————— • ————————

GAAJAR ki CHUTNEY

INGREDIENTS

1 kg/2¼ lb Carrots
675g/3 cups Sugar
250ml/1 cup White Vinegar
10g/1¾ tsp Ginger Paste (strained)
10g/1¾ tsp Garlic Paste (strained)

9g/1 Tbs Red Chilli Powder
Salt
6g/2 tsp *Jeera*/Cumin Powder
9g/1 Tbs *Garam Masala*
200g/7 oz Raisins

Preparation Time: 40 minutes
Cooking Time: 25 minutes
Maturing Time: 2 days

PREPARATION

THE CARROTS: Peel, wash and grate. Keep in the sun for 30 minutes to dry and draw out the moisture.

THE PASTES: Put the ginger and garlic pastes in muslin and squeeze out the juice. Discard the residue.

THE RAISINS: Remove the stems, refresh in water, drain and pat dry.

COOKING

Mix sugar with vinegar in *kadhai*/wok and boil until it dissolves, remove scum. Add carrots, the ginger-garlic juice and the remaining ingredients, except raisins, and simmer until the liquid has evaporated. Then add raisins and simmer until the carrots are absolutely dry. Remove and cool.

MATURING

Transfer to a sterilised jar, cover with a lid and leave it to mature for 2 days.

———————— • ————————

AAM ki CHUTNEY

INGREDIENTS

1 kg/2¼ lb Raw Mangoes
1 kg/4½ cups Sugar
100g/3 oz Onions
50g/3 Tbs Ginger Paste (strained)
20g/3½ tsp Garlic Paste (strained)
3g/1 tsp *Garam Masala*
6g/2 tsp Red Chilli Powder

15 *Chhoti Elaichi*/Green Cardamom
1.5g/½ tsp *Daalcheeni*/Cinnamon Powder
200ml/¾ cup White Vinegar
Salt
24 Almonds
100g/3 oz Raisins

Preparation Time: 30 minutes
Cooking Time: 30 minutes
Maturing Time: 2 days

PREPARATION

THE MANGOES: Peel and grate.

THE VEGETABLES: Peel, wash and grate onions. Mix with the ginger and garlic pastes, put in muslin and squeeze out the juice. Discard the residue.

THE ALMONDS: Blanch and peel.

THE CARDAMOM: Peel and discard the skins.

COOKING

Mix sugar with mangoes in a *kadhai*/wok and cook over medium heat for 10 minutes. Add the onion-ginger-garlic juice, stir, add garam masala, red chillies, cardamom seeds and cinnamon powder, stir and continue to cook until the mixture attains the consistency of a jam. Then add vinegar and salt, cook for 2-3 minutes and remove. Now, add almonds and raisins, stir and cool.

MATURING

Transfer to a sterilised jar, cover with a lid and leave it to mature for 2 days.

•

KALI MIRCH ka PAPPAD

INGREDIENTS

1Kg/2¼ lb *Urad daal ka Atta*
60g/4Tbsp Salt
15g/1 Tbsp Soda bi-carb
1g/ ½ tsp *Heeng*/Asafoetida
60g/4Tbsp Black Pepper Corns (crushed)

10g/3 tsp *Jeera*/ Cumin Seeds
30ml/ 2 Tbsp Gingelly/ Sesame Seed Oil
3g/1tsp Red Chilli Powder
250ml/1 cup (approx) Water

Yield : 150pcs (6 inch diameter)
Preparation Time: 1hr 45 minutes
Time to dry: 2 hr

PREPARATION

Sift the urad dal atta along with salt and soda bi-carb, make a bay and pour oil. Add all the other ingredients except water. Start mixing gradually till the oil is fully mixed. Add water gradually and knead to make a hard but smooth dough. Cover with a moist cloth. Divide into convenient batches and roll the dough very thin. Cut out 6-inch discs from the rolled dough with a cutter.

Arrange the pappads on a tray and leave out in the a sun for couple of hours to dry.

TO SERVE

Serve roasted in a tandoor or deep fried in oil.

ANAARDAANE ka PAPPAD

INGREDIENTS

1Kg/2¼ lbs *Urad Dal ke Atta*
60g/4 tbsp Salt

15g/ 1Tbsp Sodium bi-Carbonate
1g/½ tsp *Heeng*/Asafoetida
10g/1½ Tbsp *Jeera* / Cumin Seeds
30ml/2 Tbsp Gingelly/ Sesame Seed Oil

20g/2 Tbsp Black Pepper Corn (crushed)
60g/6 Tbsp *Anaardaana*/Pomegranate Seeds
   (crushed)
3g/1tsp Red Chilli Powder
250ml/1 cup (approx) Water

Yield : 150pcs (approx 6-inch in diameter)
Preparation Time: 1hr 45 minutes
Time to dry: 2 hrs

PREPARATION

Sift the urad dal atta along with salt and soda bi-carb, make a bay and pour oil. Add all the other ingredients except water. Start mixing gradually till the oil is fully mixed. Add water gradually and knead to make a hard but smooth dough. Cover with a moist cloth. Divide into convenient batches and roll the dough very thin. Cut out 6-inch discs from the rolled dough with a cutter. Arrange the pappads on a tray and leave them out in the sun for a couple of hours to dry.

TO SERVE

Serve roasted in a tandoor or deep fried in oil.

SUTPURRAH

INGREDIENTS

Snack

300g/11 oz *Maida*/Floor
Salt
60ml/¼ cup Cooking Oil
75g/2½ oz Yoghurt
A generous pinch of *Ajwain*/Carom Seeds

15 ml/1 The Cooking oil to brush
   dough sheets
Flour to dust
Desi Ghee/Clarified Butter to deep fry

The Filling

120/¼ lb Green Peas (boil & mash)
75g/2½ oz Potatoes (boil & grate)
25ml/2 Tbs *Desi Ghee*/Clarified Butter
2g/1 tsp *Jeera*/Cumin Seeds
10g/1" piece Ginger
4.5g/1½ tsp *Amchoor*/Mango Powder
3g/1 tsp Black Pepper
   (freshly roasted & coarsely ground)
A pinch of *Kaala Namak*/Black Rock
   Salt Powder

A pinch of *Chotti Elaich*/
   Green Cardamom Powder
A pinch of *Lavang*/Clove Powder
A pinch of *Daalcheeni*/Cinnamon Powder
Salt
2 Green Chillies (seed & finely chop)
6.5g/2 Tbs *Taaza Dhania*/Coriander (chop)

Yield: 18 Sutpurrah
Preparation Time: 1 hour
Cooking Time: 7-8 minutes for each set

PREPARATION

THE DOUGH: Sift flour and salt together in a *paraat* or on a work surface, make a bay, pour oil in it and start mixing gradually. When the oil is fully mixed, whisk and add yoghurt and ajwain and start mixing gradually. When fully mixed, add water (approx 45ml/3 Tbs), knead gently to make semi-hard dough (the dough should be harder than that for Poori and softer than that for Matthi), cover with moist cloth and keep aside for 15 minutes. Divide into 3 equal portions and make balls. Cover with moist cloth and keep aside.

THE FILLING: Heat gheen in a *kadhai*/work, add cumin, stir over medium heat until it begins to pop, add ginger and stir for a minute. Then add peas and potatoes and *bhunno*/stir-fry for a minute. Now add the remaining ingredients, except coriander, and *bhunno*/stir-fry until the mixture is completely dry. Remove, cool, add coriander, mix well and divide into 18 equal portions.

THE STUFFING: Place the balls on lightly floured surface, flatten each ball with a rolling pin into 20" × 15" rectangular sheets, and brush with oil. Fold a quarter (5") from each side, brush with oil, and fold over to obtain four layers. Dust with flour, fold the bottom third up, the top third down to obtain another 3 layers. You will now have *sut* or 7 layers. Refrigerate for 10 minutes. Remove, roll out into 15" × 6" rectangular sheets, and brush with oil. Brush with water and "divide" each piece into 6 equal portions by marking out, but not cutting, through the dough. Then place a portion of the filling one side in the middle of each of the marked out segments and fold over. Press firmly to ensure that the filling does not spill out and then carefully cut a teeny-weeny bit along the length and the sides, ensuring that the filling is not exposed. Finally cut along the marks to make 6 Sutpurrah from each sheet. Sprinkle flour on a tray, arrange Sutpurrah on it and keep aside until ready to fry.

COOKING

Heat ghee in a *kadhai*/work and begin to deep fry Sutpurrah over low heat. After the layers open up, increase to medium heat and fry until golden. Remove to absorbent paper to drain the excess fat.

TO SERVE

Place a paper doily on a silver platter, arrange the Sutpurrah on top and serve with Mint Chutney.

SAMOSA

INGREDIENTS

300g/11 oz Flour
Salt
60ml/¼ cup Cooking Oil

Cooking Oil to deep fry
Flour to dust

The Filling

450g/1 lb Corn kernels
720ml/3 cups Milk
400g/14 oz Mushrooms
60ml/¼ cup Cooking Oil
4g/2 tsp *Dhania*/Coriander Seeds
   (roasted and pounded)
4.5g/1½ tsp *Amchoor*/Mango Powder
3g/1 tsp Black Pepper (freshly roasted
   & coarsely ground)

Salt
15g/1½" piece Ginger
2 Green Chillies
6.5g/2 Tbs *Taaza Dhania*/Coriander
75g/2½ oz *Paneer*
30g/1 oz Cheddar/Processed Cheese
2g/1 tsp Rosemary (optional)

Yield: 18 Samosa
Preparation Time: 1 hour
Cooking Time: 7-8 minutes for each set

PREPARATION

THE DOUGH: Sift flour and salt together in a *paraat* or on a work surface, make a bay, pour oil in it and start mixing gradually. When the oil is fully mixed, add water (approx 90ml/6 Tbs) knead gently to make a semi-hard dough (the dough should be harder than that for *Poori* and softer than that for *Mathi*), cover with a moist cloth and keep aside for 15 minutes. Divide into 9 equal portions and make balls. Cover with a moist cloth.

THE FILLING: For the corn, put milk in a *handi*/pan, add an equal quantity (720ml/3 cups) of water and salt, bring to a boil, add the corn, cook until soft, drain, coarsely chop and keep aside. (The cooking time depends on the age of the corn. Don't be alarmed if the milk and water are completely absorbed. If the corn is soft and milky, you may need lesser quantities of milk and water. Quite obviously the corn that we experimented with was quite old and the kernels hard.)

Treat the mushrooms as described for *Subz Punjrattanee* and then finely chop. Grate *paneer* and cheese. Scrape, wash and chop ginger. Wash green chillies, slit, seed, finely chop and discard the stems. Clean, wash and finely chop coriander.

Heat oil in a *kadhai*/wok, add coriander seeds and stir over medium heat until they begin to pop. Then add the cooked corn and mushrooms, *bhunno*/stir-fry for 5-6 minutes, (be sure to stir constantly as there is the danger of the milk sticking to the bottom of the pan and burning), add *amchoor*, pepper and salt, stir, add ginger, green chillies and coriander, stir, remove and cool. Now add the remaining ingredients, mix well and divide into 18 equal portions.

THE STUFFING: Place the balls on a lightly floured surface, flatten each ball with a rolling pin into a round disc (approx 6" diameter) and cut into half. Stuff as follows: place a halve on the palm with the straight edge along the forefinger, dip the other forefinger in water, line the edges, make a cone, stuff a portion of the filling in it and seal the open end by pressing firmly. Sprinkle flour on a tray, arrange the stuffed *Samosa* on it and keep aside until ready to fry.

COOKING

Heat oil in a *kadhai*/wok and deep fry *Samosa* between low and medium heat until golden brown and crisp. Remove to absorbent paper to drain the excess fat.

TO SERVE

Place a paper doily on a silver platter, arrange the *Samosa* on top and serve with Mint Chutney and *Saunth*.

SHAHI TUKRHA

INGREDIENTS

350g/ ¾ Ib *Rabarhi* (Unsweetened)
600g/3 cup Sugar
1 drop Vetivier
3g/½ tsp Green Cardamom powder
12 slices Milk Bread
Groundnut Oil to deep fry

2 litres/8 ¹/₃ cups Milk
10g/4 tsp Almonds
5g/ 2 tsp Pistachio
1g/ 2 tsp *Zaafraan*/Saffron
Chandi-ka-Varq/Silver leaves

Yield : 12
Preparation Time : 1:15 hours
(Plus time taken for *Rabarhi*)

PREPARATION

THE RABARHI : Add 100g/ ½ cup of sugar while it is still warm and stir until dissolved. Add vetivier and stir.

THE SYRUP : Boil the remaining sugar with water (approx 300 ml/ 1¼ cups) to make a syrup of one-string consistency. Add cardamom powder and stir.

THE BREAD : Slice off the crust and trim the edges to make discs. Heat oil in a *kadhai* and deep fry over low heat until golden brown and crisp.

THE MILK : Bring to a boil in a large, flat, thick-bottomed *handi*, remove and reserve 15ml/1 Tbs to dissolve saffron.

THE *TUKRHA* : Immerse the fried bread in the remaining milk, the slices at least an inch a part. Return the *handi* to heat and simmer until the milk is absorbed, turning once in between with a spatula without breaking the bread. Remove from heat and pour on the warm syrup.

THE NUTS : Blanch almonds and pistachio, cool, remove the skin and cut into slivers.

THE SAFFRON : Dissolve in the reserved milk while it is still warm.

ASSEMBLING

Arrange the soaked *Tukrha* on a silver platter, spread *Rabarhi* on top, garnish with nuts and sprinkle saffron.

TO SERVE

Cover the *Shahi Tukrha* with *Varq* and serve warm.

Note : The alternative and just as tasty method is to serve the *Shahi Tukrha* cold. Do *not* soak in milk, pour on the warm sugar syrup on the crisp bread, spread *Rabarhi* on top, garnish with nuts, sprinkle saffron and refrigerate. Remove at the time of service, cover with *Varq* and serve.

———————— • ————————

KESARI KHEER

INGREDIENTS

1.5 litres Milk
75g Basmati Rice
15g *Desi Ghee*/Clarified Butter
125g Sugar
5g *Chhoti Elaichi*/Green Cardamom Powder

20g Almonds
15g Raisins
1g *Zaafraan*/Saffron
30ml Milk

Yield: 1kg
Preparation Time: 1:20 hours
Cooking Time: 45 minutes

PREPARATION

THE RICE: Pick, wash in running water, drain, reserve in water for an hour and drain.

THE ALMONDS: Blanch, cool, remove the skin and split.

THE SAFFRON: Crush saffron threads with a pestle, reserve in lukewarm milk and then make a paste.

COOKING

Boil milk in a *handi*/pan and remove. Heat ghee in a separate handi, add rice and *bhunno*/stir-fry until it begins to colour (approx 4-5 minutes). Transfer the milk and bring to a boil, stirring constantly (to ensure that the rice does not stick). Reduce to low heat and simmer, mashing the rice with the ladle until of custard consistency. Then add sugar and stir until dissolved. Now add the remaining ingredients and stir for a minute.

TO SERVE

Remove to a silver bowl and serve hot.

———————— • ————————

MALPUA

INGREDIENTS

100g *Suji*/Semolina
250g *Khoya*/Reduced milk
100g Flour

7.5g *Saunf*/Fennel Seeds
Desi Ghee to shallow fry Malpua

Serves: 12
Preparation Time: 1 hour
Cooking Time: 30 minutes

PREPARATION

THE SEMOLINA: Pick, wash in running water, drain and reserve in fresh water for 35-40 minutes.

THE KHOYA: Cover in enough lukewarm water and reserve until ready to make the batter.

THE BATTER: Drain the semolina and khoya. Sift flour. Mash the khoya on the work surface with the base of the palm to remove granules. Mix semolina with khoya, add flour and fennel seeds, mix well to make a batter and divide into 12 equal portions.

COOKING

To prepare the sauce, put apricot purée in a saucepan, add sugar, lemon juice and 400ml of water, bring to a boil, reduce to low heat and simmer, stirring contantly, for 5 minutes. Remove, pass through a fine mesh soup strainer into a separate saucepan, return sauce to heat and simmer until of spoon coating consistency (approx 5 minutes). Remove and keep aside.

To make the "omelette", spread a portion of the batter into a pancake of 5½" diameter in a non stick frying pan. As it begins to cook, spread a little desi ghee around the periphery and shallow fry, turning once, until light golden. Remove to absorbent paper to drain any excess fat. Repeat the process with the remaining portions of the batter.

GAAJAR ka HALWA

INGREDIENTS

2¼ lb/1kg Carrots (grate)
4¼ cups/1 litre Milk
200g/7 oz Sugar
7 Tbs/100g *Desi Ghee*/Clarified Butter
1 tsp/3g *Chotti Elaichi*/Green
    Cardamom Powder

16 Almonds (blanch, cool, peel & split)
10 Pistachio (blanch, cool, peel
    & cut into slivers)
24 Raisins
2 oz/60g *Khoya*/Reduced milk (grate)

Yield: 1kg/2¼ lb
Preparation Time: 2 hours
Cooking Time: 45 minutes

COOKING

Boil milk in a *kadhai*/wok, add the grated carrots, reduced to medium heat and cook, stirring constantly, until carrots are tender and most of the liquid has evaporated. Then add sugar and stir until dissolved and the liquid evaporates. Now add ghee and *bhunno*/stir-fry for 3-4 minutes. Remove, add cardamom, and stir. Garnish with khoya, almonds, pistachio and raisins.

———————•———————

KULFI MEDLEY

INGREDIENTS

6 litres/25 cups Milk

1.5 litres/6½ cups Cream

The Cardamom & Rose Kulfi

90ml/6 Tbs Rose Syrup
10 Egg Yolks (beat)
175g/6 oz Sugar

3g/1 tsp *Chhoti Elaichi*/
    Green Cardamom Powder

The Mango Kulfi

350ml/13 oz Mango Purée (canned)
8 Egg Yolks (beat)

150g/5 oz Sugar

The Fig & Honey Kulfi

120/4 oz *Anjeer*/Figs (dried; chop)
120ml/½ cup Honey

10 Egg Yolks
120g/4 oz Sugar

The Almond Tuilles

4 Egg Whites (beat lightly)
90g/3 oz Castor Sugar
90g/3 oz Flour (sift)

2 drops Almond Essence
24 Almond Flakes

Serves: 4
Preparation Time: 5 minutes
Cooking Time: 2 hours

PREPARATION

THE RABARHI: Put milk in a *kadhai*/wok, bring to a boil and stir constantly for 30 minutes or until reduced to a third. Remove, cool and divide into 3 equal portions.

THE ROSE 'N' CARDAMOM KULFI: Put a portion of rabarhi in a bowl, add 600ml/2½ cups of cream and cardamom powder, and mix gently. Start whisking the egg and sugar mixture over medium heat on a double boiler. When it acquires a creamy consistency, stir-in the rabarhi, and continue whisking until it comes to just under a boil. Remove and cool. When the kulfi mixture cools down to room temperature, stir-in rose syrup and stir until fully incorporated. Now put the mixture in the gelato machine, ice-cream maker (the one that churns in the freezer of a refrigerator) or the hand operated ice cream bucket (apparently an electric powered version of the contraption is also available) and churn until set. You can also put the mixture in kulfi moulds and freeze them in the traditional matka with ice and rock salt.

THE MANGO KULFI: Put a portion of rabarhi in a bowl, add 300ml/1¼ cups of cream and mix gently. Follow the procedure for Rose 'n' Cardamom Kulfi, replacing rose syrup with mango purée.

THE FIG 'N' HONEY KULFI: Put a portion of rabarhi in a bowl, add the remaining cream and mix gently. Follow the procedure for Rose 'n' Cardamom Kulfi, replacing figs and honey syrup with mango purée.

THE ALMOND TUILLES: Mix sugar, flour and essence with egg white and beat lightly to remove lumps. Reserve for an hour. Divide into 4 equal portions and spread each portion like a pancake (6" diameter) on a baking tray and bake in a pre-heated (250 °F) for 2 minutes. Remove, sprinkle the almond flakes and bake for another minute. Remove, wrap around a metal bowl of the shape you like best and cool. Remove the bowl.

TO SERVE

Put a scoop of each kulfi in an almond tuille and serve with mango (or any other fruit) sauce.

———————————•———————————

PHIRNI

INGREDIENTS

1 litre Milk
50g Basmati Rice
250g Sugar
1g *Zaafraan*/Saffron

4.5g *Chhoti Elaichi*/Green Cardamom Powder
2 drops *Ittar*/Rosewater Concentrate
12 Pistachio
12 Almonds

Serves: 4
Preparation Time: 40 minutes
Cooking Time: 15 minutes

PREPARATION

THE RICE: Pick, wash in running water and soak for 30 minutes. Drain, put in a blender, add water (approx 30ml) and make a fine paste.

THE SAFFRON: Soak in 15 ml of lukewarm water and then crush with a pestle or the back of a spoon to make a paste.

THE NUTS: Blanch pistachio and almonds separately, cool, remove the skin and cut into slivers.

THE SHIKORAS: Rinse in running water and then immerse in a handi full of water for 25 minutes. Remove and pat dry.

COOKING

Boil the remaining milk in a *handi*/pan, add the rice paste and sugar stirring constantly with a whisk. Reduce to low heat and cook, stirring constantly (to ensure no lumps are formed), until the mixture becomes thick and is reduced to a custard consistency. Then add saffron, cardamom and ittar, stir and remove.

ASSEMBLING

Pour equal quantities of Phirni in the shikoras (or glass bowls), garnish with pistachio and almond slivers, cool and refrigerate until set.

TO SERVE

Remove shikoras from refrigerator and serve cold.

—————— • ——————

BADAAM ka HALWA

INGREDIENTS

500g/1 lb 2 oz Almonds
50g/¼ cup *Desi Ghee*/Clarified Butter
500g/1 lb 2 oz *Khoya*/Reduced Milk
500g/1 lb 11 oz Sugar
480ml/2 cups Milk

1g/2 tsp *Zaafraan*/Saffron
3g/1 tsp *Chhoti Elaichi*/
    Green Cardamom Powder
A few drops of Almond Essence
24 Pistachio

Yield: 1.5 Kg/3 lb 5 oz
Preparation Time: 45 minutes
Cooking Time: 10 minutes

PREPARATION

THE ALMONDS: Blanch, cool and remove skin. Heat half the ghee (25g/2 Tbs) in a frying pan, add the almonds and fry over medium heat until light golden. Drain, cool, transfer to a blender and make a coarse paste.

THE KHOYA: Grate.

THE SAFFRON: Crush with a pestle or with the back of a spoon, reserve in 30ml/2 Tbs of lukewarm milk and then grind into a paste at the time of cooking.

THE PISTACHIO: Blanch, cool, remove skin and cut into slivers.

COOKING

Heat the remaining ghee in a *kadhai*/wok, add khoya, *bhunno*/stir-fry over medium heat until lightly coloured, add sugar, stir for a minute, add the remaining milk, stir, add the almond paste, stir, add the saffron paste, stir and then *bhunno*/stir-fry for 5-6 minutes. Remove, add cardamom and stir.

TO SERVE

Remove to silver bowl, garnish with pistachio slivers and serve hot.

MASALAS

Spices have, for centuries, commanded a unique position in international trade. The irony is that, with Indians, familiarity with spices has bred contempt, not respect. Spices are not given their due. The truth is there is nothing more important in the culinary universe than spices. Colour, aroma and taste—the quintessence of gourmet foods—would not have been possible without spices.

There is, thus, a great need to remove the various misconceptions about spices. Foremost, spices are not synonymous with chillies. Then, there is this belief among most cooks that bunging in huge quantities of spices enhances the taste and flavour. Nothing could be farther from the truth.

The key is in the balance. Balanced spicing. As my Grandmother, Ram Rakhi, once told my mother: "Bol-chaal ki bhaasha mein, namak aur mirch ko saath rakha jaata hai aur mirch-masale mein farq kiya jaata hai". We often tend to forget that the splendours of Indian cuisine derive from therapeutic and aesthetic use of spices and not their abuse.

When the Queen of Sheba visited the court of Solomon, she perfumed herself with the aromatic spices of India. Some historians maintain that the Roman Empire plunged headlong into decline because the Caesars squandered their resources on expensive spices from India.

However, the most amazing legend is preserved by the Arab spice traders. They believed that the mythological bird, the Phoenix, could rise from the ashes only because it constructed its pyre-nest with cinnamon sticks! They had the world believe that to obtain the aromatic spices of Hind, they had to combat the fierce bird to accomplish their mission, and then, for millennia, used this "bloody battle" as a pretext to hike the prices.

Growing tired of con, the Europeans decided to embark on exploratory voyages of their own to provide exotica to their spice-hungry consumers. And, the rest, as they say, is history. From Columbus mistaking America for the East Indies to Vasco da Gama reaching Cragnore!

The world may have changed much since then, but Malabar remains the treasure trove of spicy exotica. Obviously, this verdant coast is blessed with a climate and soil conditions that allow spices and herbs to not just grow, but grow in abundance. And this is the reason why gourmet from across the globe are drawn to Kerala.

If spices are the basis of Indian cooking, the blending of these spices to make a *garam masala* is the essence of it. Each spice in the melange has a specific purpose to perform. It is therefore important to be good *masalchi* before one can become a good chef. To quote Grandma again, "Masale mazzedaar toh sub ko lagte hein, par inki kutayi pisayi mein naani yaad aa jati hai. Aankh-naak seh paani nikalne lagta hai."

It is advisable to try out various combinations fearlessly—so long as they are balanced and each spice (in the combination) is in harmony with the others. Before that, however, a clear understanding of each and every spice is imperative. Accordingly, the proportions of spices can be changed as the seasons change. For example, in the hot summer months, reduce the quantities of mace and nutmeg—they can lead to a nosebleed.

There are as many versions of the garam masala as there are chefs. However, in general, some garam masala are tongue-tingling 'hot' (those with cloves and pepper), while others are only aromatic (cinnamon, mace, cardamom, etc). Garam masala is used sparingly or it will put the 'body on fire' It is almost always introduced toward the end of cooking a delicacy. Often it is used as a garnish—sprinkled over cooked food to provide aromatic flavouring at the time of service.

It would be absurd to reduce every dish to the lowest common denominator by using the same combination for every dish. The secret of good cooking is to make a separate garam masala for each dish.

It cannot be denied that spices in their raw form have certain disadvantages. Whole or ground spices do not always impart their flavour readily and when we use proprietary, pre-ground spices, much of the aromatic quality is lost. This is the result of the volatility of essential oils and oleo resins which are the life of the spice.

———————— • ————————

GARAM MASALA

INGREDIENTS

90g/3oz *Jeera*/Cumin Seeds
75g/2½ oz *Motti Elaichi*/
   Black Cardamom Seeds
75g/2½oz Black Peppercorns
45g/1½oz *Chotti Elaichi*/Green Cardamom

20 sticks *Daalcheeni*/Cinnamon (1")
20g/¾ oz *Javitri*/Mace
20g/¾ oz *Shahi Jeera*/Black Cumin Seeds
15g/½ oz *Tej Patta*/Bay Leaves
15g/½ oz Dry Rose petals

30g/1 oz *Dhania*/Coriander Seeds
30g/1 oz *Saunf*/Fennel Seeds
20g/¾ oz *Lavang*/Cloves

15g/½ oz Ginger powder
3 *Jaiphal*/Nutmeg

Yield: approx 450g/1 lb

PREPARATION

Put all ingredients, except ginger powder, in mortar and pound with pestle to make fine powder. Transfer to clean, dry bowl, add ginger powder and mix well. Sift and store in sterilised, dry and airtight container.

———————————— • ————————————

AROMATIC GARAM MASALA

INGREDIENTS

175g/6 oz *Chotti Elaichi*/Green Cardamom
125g/41/2oz *Jeera*/Cumin Seeds
125g/41/2oz Black Peppercorns

20 sticks *Daalcheeni*/Cinnamon (1")
20g/3/4 oz *Lavang*/Cloves
2 *Jaiphal*/Nutmeg

Yield : approx 450g/1 lb

PREPARATION

Put all ingredients in mortar and pound with pestle to make fine powder. Sift and store in sterilised, dry and airtight container.

———————————— • ————————————

CHAAT MASALA

INGREDIENTS

65g/2¼ oz *Jeera*/Cumin Seeds
65g/2¼ oz Black Peppercorns
60g/2 oz *Kaala Namak*/Black Salt *
30g/1 oz Dry *Pudhina*/Mint Leaves

5g/1 tsp *Heeng*/Asafoetida*
4g/³/₄ tsp *Tartari*/Tartric Acid*
    (crystalline granular form)
150g/5¼ oz *Amchoor*/Mango Powder

5g/2 tsp *Ajwain*/Carom Seeds

20g/³/₄ oz *Sounth*/Ginger Powder
20g/³/₄ oz *Peeli Mirch*/Yellow Chilli Powder

Yield : approx 450g/1 lb

PREPARATION

Put all ingredients, except mango powder, salt, ginger powder and yellow chilli powder, in mortar and pound with pestle to make fine powder. Transfer to clean, dry bowl, add remaining ingredients and mix well. Sift and store in sterilised, dry and airtight container.

———————— • ————————

TANDOORI CHAAT MASALA

INGREDIENTS

50g/ 1¾ oz *Jeera*/Cumin Seeds
50g/1¾ oz Black Peppercorns
50g/1¾ oz *Kaala Namak*/Black Salt*
30g/1 oz Dry *Pudhina*/Mint leaves
20g/³/₄ oz *Kasoori Methi*/Fenugreek
30 *Chotti Elaichi*/Green Cardamom
15 *Lavang*/Cloves
5 sticks *Daalcheeni*/Cinnamon (1-inch)

5g/2 tsp *Ajwain*/Carom Seeds
5g/1 tsp *Heeng*/Asafoetida*
4g/¾ tsp *Tartari* (Tartric Acid)*
2g/½ tsp *Javitri*/Mace
125g/4½ oz *Amchoor*/Mango Powder
20g/¾ oz *Sounth*/Ginger Powder
20g/¾ oz *Peeli Mirch*/Yellow Chilli Powder

Yield : approx 450g/1 lb

PREPARATION

Put all ingredients, except mango powder, salt, ginger powder and yellow chilli powder, in mortar and pound with pestle to make fine powder. Transfer to a clean, dry bowl, add remaining ingredients and mix well. Sift and store in sterilised, dry and airtight container.

* Break into small pieces, if using grinder.

INDEX